3D Coach is an important resou   !oesn't
matter what level of sport you are   beside
your Bible as a supplement and gu   ...eaningful way.
Jeff's stories are profound, his hon   ...g and his wisdom and teaching on point. I will be reading and rereading this inspirational book with the
same passion I study game film! I believe it will help you truly win, as it gives
you lots to think about and a clear vision of what 3D coaching is all about!

Jane Albright
Head Women's Basketball Coach, University of Nevada, Las Vegas

Something happened to me when I read *3D Coach*. My spirit was awakened. Jeff
had me walking in his shoes as a coach, as an athlete and as a father. His stories caused me to look at the Bible in a different light. All of my coaching
thoughts, questions and challenges now make sense. Jeff has given coaches
a blueprint to become a better coach, father, husband and Christian. This
book will be on my desk to inspire me and guide me daily. Thank you, Jeff.

John Cook
Head Volleyball Coach, University of Nebraska

3D coaching is not simply another philosophy of coaching. It is a paradigm
shift in purpose that leads to the outcomes we all desire, but often fail to
achieve. As a Division I wrestling coach, I can truly say that this shift has
influenced our staff, our athletes and me in a dynamic way. This material is
hands down the best I have ever seen for coaches who truly want to have an
impact and to pursue excellence.

Heath Eslinger
Head Wrestling Coach, University of Tennessee at Chattanooga

Having worked with Jeff for many years in coaching ministry I knew his
heart and his teachings would be greatly beneficial to many.

Rod Olson
Founder, Coaches of Excellence
Author, *The Legacy Builder*

THE HEART OF A COACH® SERIES

THE FELLOWSHIP OF CHRISTIAN ATHLETES

3D COACH

JEFF DUKE

WITH **CHAD BONHAM**

Regal

For more information and
special offers from Regal Books, email us at
subscribe@regalbooks.com

Published by Regal
From Gospel Light
Ventura, California, U.S.A.
www.regalbooks.com
Printed in the U.S.A.

Library of Congress Cataloging-in-Publication Data
Duke, Jeff.
3D coach : capturing the heart behind the jersey / Jeff Duke.
pages cm
ISBN 978-0-8307-6969-8 (trade paper : alk. paper) 1. Coaching (Athletics)
2. Coaching (Athletics)—Religious aspects—Christianity. I. Title.
GV711.D85 2014
796.07'7—dc23
2014010045

Rights for publishing this book outside the U.S.A. or in non-English languages
are administered by Gospel Light Worldwide, an international not-for-profit
ministry. For additional information, please visit www.glww.org,
email info@glww.org, or write to Gospel Light Worldwide,
1957 Eastman Avenue, Ventura, CA 93003, U.S.A.

To order copies of this book and other Regal products in bulk quantities,
please contact us at 1-800-446-7735.

DEDICATION

I dedicate this book to my wife, Dana, my children—four boys Bo, Cam, Matt and Mark—and my parents, Carl and Ginny Duke.

Dana, the rock and stability of our lifelong journey together as husband and wife, mother of our four sons, and my best friend. You make life so enjoyable and so complete. I am so in love!

Bo, Cam, Matt, Mark, my greatest legacy. . . children who are on their own transformational purpose journey. I love being your dad.

Carl and Ginny Duke, parents who forever modeled how to love God and one another. . . forever grateful.

CONTENTS

FOREWORD

By Bobby Bowden

This is a story of a journey, one that every coach should take: a journey that should ultimately identify his own calling as a coach.

I was introduced to Jeff by a prominent booster who wanted me to meet a young high school coach from his hometown church. It was evident from this initial meeting that Jeff understood the dynamic influence a coach could have on the lives of athletes. From his earliest days as a graduate assistant coach, it became evident to me that he should serve as the FCA facilitator for our team. All of my coaches had an off-field responsibility, but this was the one whom I knew could have lifelong impact on our players. I did not take this assignment lightly. I wanted those I appointed to be committed to this endeavor. It was never a requirement for our players to attend the weekly FCA huddle, but I knew they would try it out if our coaching staff emphasized its importance. I so admired Jeff and his wife, Dana, in the way they engaged the players and made FCA an integral part of our program.

After a few years, Jeff left Florida State and became the first FCA field representative in North Florida and South Georgia. Our families have stayed close and in contact for over three decades. As I have witnessed Jeff on his journey, both in the victories and struggles, I have clearly seen him reach this unique position where he can now help coaches identify their purpose and their calling as they travel their own journeys.

Jeff is an excellent coach and has used his coaching expertise, life experiences and academic prowess to help other coaches identify and develop all three dimensions of what it takes to become a great coach in the twenty-first century! *3D Coach* is a must-read for all coaches of any sport at any level.

FOREWORD

By Tommy Bowden

Jeff and I were introduced in the summer of 1978 as graduate assistant coaches for Florida State University. From the first time we met while cutting film in a small, graduate assistant coach's office, we have become lifetime friends. His wife, Dana, and my wife, Linda, have stayed in close contact ever since. Our careers diverted after a few years at Florida State but our friendship has grown ever deeper. Through the births of our children, marriages, career changes and even the deaths of extended family members, we have encouraged and uplifted each other.

Whenever we get together, conversation always evolves into the ever-increasing role of the coach in our culture today. Jeff and I have the same philosophy—that coaching creates a legacy for all those influenced by a coach. The question begs a response: What type of legacy are we talking about here? It has been so enjoyable to see Jeff develop this into strategy for coaches to use today. The 3Dimensional Coaching principles will help them cultivate all areas of the athlete's life: body, soul and spirit.

My dad and I have always understood and implemented this concept, but now it can be identified and engaged by all coaches. It is the fulfillment of understanding and living out your purpose beyond the game. It will give stability and contentment in the ups and downs of the coaching profession. *3D Coach* is Jeff's story. But as you are reading it, you will begin to contemplate your story . . . your influence. . . your legacy.

PURPOSE STATEMENT

The role of the coach has obtained idolized proportions in our society today. Sports, in the American culture, have become an icon of popularity from the very young to the elderly. Up to 50 million adolescents will have participated on an athletic team before entering their adult years. In fact, we now spend more time watching, reading or actively being involved in sport activities than any of life's other discretional domains. Because of this cultural focus, the coach has become the point person for this societal phenomenon. In fact, research reflects the coach as one of the most influential persons in American life. The coach now takes on the role of an authority figure for much of the traditional American ethos (i.e., commitment to goals, team-first attitudes, excellence of cause, life attributions, etc.). For many reasons, these value systems are being lost or de-emphasized in the home environment. It is with this premise that we, as sport coaching educators, are making a concerted effort to come alongside the coaches' fraternity to help encourage, educate and produce the next generation of coaches to meet the demand of our sport culture in this changing sport landscape.

The need for higher education to provide a quality program and also direction for coaches, sport administrators, athletes and the public regarding the necessary skills, knowledge and research is now of utmost importance. This needed educational expansion, from a sub-discipline to a discipline, will allow improved standards related to the care, health, performance and safety of athletes. Because coaches are teachers, their influence with athletes in many ways has attribution effects in many facets of life. Coaches today must have resources to improve knowledge and skills to meet changing expectations on and off the field.

Over 100 sports organizations have agreed that a core body of knowledge to develop scientific and practical competencies is now identified. This body has been outlined and identified in the published *National Standards for Athletic Coaches*. A highly acclaimed accreditation agency, the National Council for Accreditation of Coaching Education (NCACE), has been established to give direction and guidance to the pursuit of key deliverables in coaching education institutions. The first (and most important) domain in these national standards is developing and implementing an athlete-centered coaching philosophy in the midst of a performance-based culture. This balance is very rarely achieved, with only a small percentage of coaches able to maximize the positive lifelong benefits of sport participation for *each* athlete and still produce a winning culture at their respective institutions.

The initial inroad into these coaching perspectives is now a central focus of the international sport ministry organization Fellowship of Christian Athletes (FCA). FCA is using the 3Dimensional teaching and learning strategies as a visual reference for coaches to identify their coaching style (or philosophy) as related to biblical principles and underscored by current research. The teaching modules allow coaches to witness a transformational coaching style that develops a higher-producing athlete through the transformed life of the coach. This is facilitated by 3Dimensional Coaching workshops and underscored by online training modules. This material has received rave reviews from coaches and administrators at all levels of education (public schools, private schools, colleges, universities and major sports organizations). The outcome of the workshop will be the beginning or the continuing personal transformational process of the coach in gaining or enhancing the joy of being *called to coach*.

It is with unmatched joy from an FCA staff perspective to witness the coach and his or her family fulfilling God's purpose to be a great coach with an even *greater* message!

INTRODUCTION

Take a look at the *New York Times* bestsellers list. You'll probably see a lot of familiar names—politicians, broadcasters, athletes, award-winning novelists, mega-church pastors, TV stars, etc. I am not one of those people. So why are you reading this book? There must be something that would justify the investment of time and money it takes to attentively read through 160 or so pages of text.

A quick Google search might do the trick. But guess what? You won't find much there either—probably something about my connection to the Fellowship of Christian Athletes, lecturer at the University of central Florida, or perhaps my early years as an assistant football coach at Florida State, or lately, as a clinician and presenter of 3Dimensional Coaching, but nothing that will knock your socks off. My picture doesn't hang in any hall of fame. I've never coached in the NFL, much less in a Super Bowl.

So getting back to the reason why you are holding *3D Coach*. It's possible that someone gave this book to you because it's about coaching and you're a coach. Or perhaps you picked it up because the title jumped out at you and, again, because you're a coach. That's pretty much the bottom line here. You're a coach and so am I.

This book isn't your typical coaching book. It's not about the science of game planning or some fresh new offensive or defensive schemes. It's not about conditioning and training or secrets to helping your athletes physically reach their potential. All of those things are important. All of those things are necessary if you want to be a successful coach.

But *3D Coach* is about going deeper. It's about seeing your athletes in three dimensions—body, mind and spirit. It's about a journey that we are *all* on whether we realize it or not. It's about the art of coaching. It's about discovering what your true purpose is as a coach and rediscovering the joy you may have lost along the way. It's about seeing the coaching profession through the eyes of Jesus Christ—the one I refer to as the "Master Coach."

As you read this book, keep in mind that my story is really no different than yours. It is my prayer that you will be able to relate to my struggles as a young coach and the difficulties I faced as I painstakingly began to understand what it really means to be a 3D Coach. For some of you, the things I've learned on my journey will validate what you've been doing or what you've wanted to do differently. For others, my story will, hopefully, challenge you to make positive changes.

It took me nearly 20 years of trial and error and another 10 years of learning and implementation to get where I am today. And I'm still learning! In fact, I believe that the learning process continues until the day you finally hang up the whistle for good.

I'm so glad that you've decided to join me on this journey!

COACH

CAPTURING THE HEART BEHIND THE JERSEY

1

ONE FRIDAY NIGHT IN FLORIDA

High school football in Florida is a big deal. If you don't believe me, show up at any random stadium on a Friday night during the autumn months. It's not terribly different from what you might experience in the average American town. You can smell the concessions from blocks away. You can hear the marching band warming up in the distance. You can see the cheer squad practicing their routines. You can hear the crackling of the loudspeakers as the public address announcers welcome the crowd.

But here in Florida, there's a fervor among fans that tends to reach a fevered pitch like no other sport. There's an intensity among the players and coaches that is almost palpable. You can feel it in the atmosphere. High school football is serious business around these parts—and I love it.

I must admit, after all these years, I still get excited about being on the field during pregame warm-ups or getting on an old yellow-dog bus to head off to face a nearby rival. The smell of freshly cut grass and the sight of perfectly placed chalk lines get to me every time.

But there was something a little bit unusual that took place on a particular Friday night during the 2013 season. It was my first year serving as the passing coach at South Lake High School. As we were preparing for a home game against Orlando Edgewater, a young man named David Rubin closely observed our team from the sidelines.

At the time, David was going through a graduate program that I teach at the University of Central Florida. He wanted to see firsthand what my coaching philosophy looked like when enacted by an entire staff. It didn't take long for David to both see and *feel* the difference.

I introduced him to my family and then to some of the players and coaches. David would later tell me that he immediately felt like a part of the team. He was amazed to see the verbal displays of affection and encouragement. Teammates paired up for impromptu pep talks. Equipment managers hobnobbed with star athletes. Coaches smiled more often than they scowled.

"I love you, Coach!" one player told me.

"Anything I can help you with?" another player asked.

"It was mind blowing," David said, "to see firsthand the result of relational coaching."

"I want to have that memory with me forever," he later shared. "Everybody was focused on enjoying life and being with each other. It makes me that much hungrier to be the same kind of coach."

Long before David visited that game, he knew there was a better way to do things as a coach. He just didn't know what to call it. And he certainly didn't see it modeled in many other places. But by the time he left the stadium that day, David was validated. He was empowered to see athletes as people first and to truly care about their personal and spiritual needs. In fact, David had his own youth basketball game to coach that weekend and the first thing he did when he saw his players was to tell them how proud he was of them and how much he loved them.

Young people like David are seeing it. They're feeling it. They instinctively know that the old way of coaching just isn't getting it done anymore. Unfortunately, most of us coaches today coach the same way we were coached. If our coaches were primarily hard-nosed, drill sergeant types, we have probably adopted that same style throughout our coaching career. If our coaches were relationship oriented, or "players' coaches," as they are sometimes called, then we have probably leaned more towards that leadership approach.

So the question isn't, "What style of coach are you?" but rather, "Are you teachable and coachable, or are you rigid and set in your ways?"

John Wooden, the legendary UCLA basketball coach, once said, "It's what you learn after you know it all that separates the great coaches from the average ones."

Here's another way to look at it: Are you coaching based on what you have learned in the past, or are you coaching based on what your athletes need?

As Wooden conveyed, great coaches only become great when they admit that they haven't learned everything there is to learn about the profession. Great coaches continue striving for new ways to teach, to inspire and to challenge their athletes.

For the longest time, I failed to understand why I loved coaching because I was so frustrated with the daily grind that comes with the job. As with so many other coaches, I had taken a one-dimensional approach to the profession. While I tried to be a relational coach, too often I fell back on the task-oriented style of leadership that worked for a while, and that ultimately led back to unnecessary stress and aggravation. Many years later, I would identify it as "first-dimensional coaching," a method that focuses mostly on the physical aspects of sport. It is not that I ignored the emotional and spiritual needs of the athlete, but I never developed a specific strategy to coach those needs. I just hoped it would happen. That is not coaching. That is just wishing!

So, the scene that my student David experienced on a fateful Friday night in Central Florida was decades in the making. It took years of trudging along a bumpy and treacherous road. In fact, even today, I feel as if I'm just beginning to truly grasp the breadth and value of relational coaching or, as I like to call it, "capturing the heart of the athlete."

TRAINING TIME

1. What are some of the things you love most about the sport(s) you coach?
2. How were you coached as an athlete, and how have those experiences impacted the way you coach today?
3. If you were to honestly assess yourself as a coach, would you consider yourself to be teachable or more set in your ways? Give some examples of how either or both attributes have been manifested in your coaching career.
4. What are some things that you would like to change about your approach to coaching, and why?

PRAYER

Lord, thank You for blessing me with the opportunity to influence young people as a coach. Give me the desire and the energy to make whatever changes might be necessary in order to reach for a higher level of coaching.

2

BORN TO COACH

I've coached several sports throughout my career, but for the most part my coaching has been within the realm of football. From youth leagues all the way up to the college level, I've been a lifelong student of the game.

But that's not important. In fact, it doesn't really matter what sport you coach or whether it's as a JV assistant or as a professional head coach. The journey is the same. The struggles are interchangeable, and so are the rewards.

My love affair with sports started at a young age. I was born in Miami, Florida, to Carl and Ginny Duke. My father was a salesman and manager for Nabisco. My mom worked at the *Miami Herald* in the classified section.

Some of my earliest sports memories were from Thanksgiving Day football games that annually featured my parents' high school alma mater. I was also heavily influenced by University of Miami football. My dad always made sure we had season tickets and attended as many home games as we possibly could. Our presence at the Orange Bowl every New Year's Day was another significant part of my young fan experience. That iconic stadium was my sports sanctuary.

I didn't have any siblings, so when I was growing up in South Florida, my buddies acted as surrogate brothers. By the time I was five years old, I was part of some pretty massive pickup games in the park. I was always creating teams and making up plays. At the age of seven, I had already developed my first playbook.

Eventually our games moved to Haulover Beach Park on Miami Beach. We loved playing beach football. We would draw lines in the sand to represent two end zones and a sideline along the beach. The other sideline? Europe. We could go as far into the Atlantic Ocean as we wanted. For hours, we'd catch the ball, tackle each other, and run into the deep water. It was intensely competitive. But even more important, it was the most fun any kid could imagine.

My first experience with organized sports took place in the North Dade area where I played tackle football when I was eight and nine years old. I then played flag football at Palm Springs Junior High until I was 13 years old.

Amid the sports mania that enveloped our lives, my parents were diligent about church attendance. They introduced me to Christian youth leaders who mentored me and helped me grow spiritually. I always found strength, confidence and solace within the youth group experience.

Of course, none of that would have meant much had I not made a personal commitment to accept Jesus Christ as my Lord and Savior when I was 12 years old. At the time, my parents were officially becoming members of a local church. When they went to the front of the sanctuary to move their membership from our previous church to the current church, I went with them. After saying some words to the congregation, the pastor leaned down to me and asked this simple question:

"Do you know Jesus as your Lord and Savior?"

"Yes," I replied.

I really hadn't accepted Christ and asked Him to forgive my sins. But in the moment, my pride caused me to respond otherwise. After all, wasn't that what the pastor *wanted* me to say?

That night, I woke up from my sleep and started crying uncontrollably. It was there, alone in my bed, that I knew I needed a Savior. It was a very real, genuine moment in my spiritual journey. Looking back, I'm sure that my parents had been praying for me. That Sunday morning, God saw my tender heart and revealed Himself to me. I thank Him every day for my godly parents.

When I was 14 years old, I started playing football at Dade Christian High School. During that first year, I was abruptly introduced to the harsh reality of two-a-days. Playing beach football was fun, but this was something very different. After the second day of 95-degree weather and 95-percent humidity, I decided to quit playing football. I simply wasn't motivated enough to endure the intense heat and the difficult workouts. Football wasn't fun anymore.

I got home that night and my dad called me to join him in the family room. This was long before the days of the cell phone, yet somehow, Coach Mike Corbett had already contacted my dad and made him aware of my absence at practice. As I sat on a chair in the living room, Dad simply said, "Jeff, you're a Duke. Dukes don't quit. You made a commitment to that team and you're going to keep that commitment. You won't miss any more practices and you will do whatever the coach asks you to do. At the end of the season, we can reevaluate. Do you understand?"

"Yes, sir," I meekly replied.

I knew there was no use fighting it. My father's authority reigned supreme in our household and obedience was the only option. I never missed a day of practice after that. I'm glad I was compelled to stick it out. If my father had allowed me to quit, I would have missed out on some incredible experiences. I grew to adore Coach Corbett. As I look back, I now know why. He was a true 3D Coach. He motivated me. He gave me great confidence. He was always full of joy.

And he masterfully created an atmosphere that allowed for strong team cohesion. Just writing this makes me want to call Coach and say, "Thanks."

Interceptions and the Law of Averages

I was never a great athlete, but I was pretty good. In fact, I made varsity as a freshman and saw increased playing time during my years on the team. At a recent Christmas gathering, my four boys were with us at home. When you get a bunch of guys together who love sports, there are typically stories about how good an athlete you were. It wasn't long before one of my sons asked the loaded question, "Well, Dad, how good were you?"

With the entire family, my wife, Dana, included, sitting around the living room, I had to take a few moments to think up something that might give my kids a glimpse into my glory days on the football field. Finally it came to me.

"Well, my junior year of high school, I led Dade County with nine interceptions," I proudly proclaimed.

Dade County is a big county. There are a lot of athletes who play football and many who go on to play at the collegiate level. Surely that was enough to appease my sons' curiosity.

"Dad, can you prove it?" one of my boys chimed in.

Is my word not good enough? I privately thought.

Apparently, it wasn't. So my wife recommended we look through my old yearbook to see if confirmation of my on-the-field exploits might be found there. She ran off to retrieve it and quickly returned to the living room with what would hopefully provide some hard evidence. It's scary enough to go back and look at old yearbooks, but it's even scarier when you're trying to prove that one of your old football stories is actually true.

We thumbed through the pages and finally came to the sports section. Remember, I told them I had nine interceptions that year. But when we looked at the page it said very clearly: "Jeff Duke led Dade County in interceptions with six."

You know the old saying, "The older we get the better we were." Apparently what I had done was to add one interception for every 10 years I've been out of high school. In fact, I'm about two years away from increasing that season total to 10!

I've coached football long enough to figure out how it happened. When you're a slow defensive back (and I was definitely slow), opposing coaches know whom they can pick on. I probably had the ball thrown in my direction a thousand times. So I had a lot of opportunities to intercept a few passes here and there. I led the county in interceptions due to the law of averages.

"What Do You Really Want to Do?"

After graduating from Dade Christian, I left Florida to play NAIA football at Carson-Newman College. Since my brief time at the school, it has been renamed Carson-Newman University and competes at the NCAA Division 2 level. I only lasted a short time on the team before hanging up my cleats for good.

I came back home and landed at the University of South Florida in Tampa. My football career was over but my search for the perfect career path was just beginning. Something infinitely more important happened during these early young adult years. It was a Sunday night when my best friend, Bob Silsby, and I went to church for the express purpose of enjoying the talents of two special guests. A young lady named Dana and her sister, Joy, had traveled from their rural hometown of Plant City to play guitar and banjo for the congregation.

There they were in their miniskirts and boots singing "The Baptism of Jesse Taylor." I'd like to say it was a major spiritual event in my life, but I have to be honest and say there wasn't much of anything spiritual about it at all. I was hooked. After their performance, we motioned for them to come and sit by us on the pews. They did and the rest is history. Dana and I got married during my senior year of college and we've been together now for over 30 years!

It was actually a year earlier when my career plans started to take shape. As my junior year in college approached, it was time for me to declare my major. I met with my advisor to discuss my future career path. As with most meetings of this nature, it started with a simple question.

"What do you want to do?" she asked.

"I want to coach," I quickly replied.

"That's nice," she replied, trying not to sound patronizing. "What do you *really* want to do?"

Without hesitation and with great conviction I once again responded, "Ma'am, I want to coach."

"We don't have a degree for that here," she retorted. "You'll have to pick something else."

Most certainly, other coaches of that era received the same advice I was given that day: Pursue a Physical Education major. And that's exactly what I did. For some reason I couldn't explain at the time, I had a strong desire to stay deeply involved with sports far beyond the place my limited athletic ability could take me.

My future father-in-law was a high school principal and gave me some great advice. He recommended that I get a minor in both Math and Science. I would need to get certified if I wanted to teach and expand my job opportunities beyond coaching. After completing my undergraduate work at a high school just outside Tampa, I graduated from USF and was quickly hired as a coach and biology teacher at Zephyrhills High School.

I knew immediately why I loved coaching. It puts you in a position of leadership. People listen to you. Students walk past you in the hallways and say, "Hi, Coach!" There's a sense of respect that immediately accompanies the title. So I dove in headfirst and with every bit of energy I could muster. I coached cross-country in the morning and JV football in the afternoon. I was the head JV basketball coach in the winter and the head track coach in the spring. I also coached spring football, which took up a considerable amount of time as well.

But I loved every exhausting minute of it!

The First Nudge

It wasn't a power trip, but there was something special about that first year and the realization that coaches—perhaps more than any other youth leadership position—can gain the undivided attention of young people quickly. Furthermore, kids will do what a coach asks them to do most of the time.

It was during my first year at Zephyrhills High School when that principle revealed itself in a unique way. I wanted to be a really good basketball coach. My JV team was about to open the season with a home game on a Saturday night. During preseason practices I prepared them to play well—to defend well. Earlier that week, I gathered them together for a post-practice meeting. I had come up with a unique way of getting them ready for that first game.

"Team," I said in my best coach's voice, "this Friday night, I want you to bring your sleeping bags up to the gym. We're going to spend the night here. We'll have pizza and Coke and just hang out and have a good time."

About a dozen pairs of eyes focused intently on me. Their ears attentively listened to every word I said as I explained myself.

"We're going to own this floor!" I continued. "Nobody is going to come into *our* gym and beat us!"

That was all it took. A bunch of 14- and 15-year-old kids were sold. And guess what? They all showed up on Friday night with their sleeping bags ready to eat some pizza and sleep on a hardwood floor. It didn't seem to matter that there was no air conditioning and the Florida atmosphere was warm and humid. All we had was a giant ceiling fan to occasionally generate enough breeze to cool us a little.

Around 10:30 that night, I turned out the gym lights and tried to get the boys to settle down and go to sleep. I'm not sure what I was thinking, but somehow I didn't anticipate that they would do what kids do. True to form, they started acting crazy and stupid. They were running around, goofing off and jumping on the bleachers.

I'd had all I could take. I got up and hustled to turn on the gym lights. The first thing I noticed was kind of interesting. I'd never realize all the different creatures that crawl around on a Florida gym floor at night. But in the moment, I was too perturbed by the kids to let the sight of insects and small reptiles shake me from my mission.

I stood at center court and yelled at the top of my lungs, "All of you guys get over here!"

I'll never forget what happened next. They immediately quieted down as I had them sit around the center circle at half court. As I looked out at the kids, I was still a little mad at them. Up until that point, I had tried my best to follow God. I understood what Christ had done on the cross for me. I had made that very strong profession of faith when I was 12 years old. And now I was as a Christian coach in my early 20s. I was about 10 years into my

Christian walk and just a year or two into my journey as a coach. I knew that somehow these things ought to work together, but I just couldn't make the connection.

For the first time, in a hot, sweaty gym on a Friday night with a bunch of JV basketball players, God nudged me and the Holy Spirit revealed a powerful truth to me. It was if He was speaking these words to my heart:

Look at the eyes of these kids. They listen to every word you say. You told them that sleeping on a maple wood floor was good for them, and they bought into it! Every one of them bought into it! They believed you when you told them this would make them better basketball players. Are you going to tell them about Me?

I'll never forget that night, although I can't recall exactly what I said in the moment. I muttered some words about how God had a call on their lives and I told them that God loved them. I don't know how good my speech was, but I suddenly felt a strong conviction that this thing called coaching and this walk with Christ were supposed to run parallel. In fact, for the first time it was revealed to me that both roads were meant to become one and the same.

I didn't know where to go, where to turn for advice on how to combine my dual purposes into one cohesive reality. I felt out of place going back to my church and talking about it. I had this competitive nature and it seemed to be in conflict with my Christian nature. I wanted to do well. I wanted my 14-year-old athletes to win while somehow maintaining Christ-like attributes.

So during that first year at Zephyrhills High School, I gave everything I had to becoming the best cross-country, basketball, football and track coach I could be. Finally, the athletic calendar came to a close. I was beat up and tired as I walked into the house after the season-ending state track meet.

Dana and I had only been married a little over one year and she was already tired of the constant sports coaching.

"This is crazy," she told me as we sat in the living room. "This four-sports-a-year thing isn't working. Pick one or pick me."

She was right. I had worked so hard that year that I had barely given myself time to breathe, much less enjoy the things about coaching that I so dearly loved. So I dropped all the other sports and picked one: football.

||||||||||||||||||||||||||||||||||||||||||||||||||||||||||||||||||||||||||||||||||||||||||||||||||||||

I really loved this journey I was on,
but a nagging thought continued to fester:
There has to be a better way.

||||||||||||||||||||||||||||||||||||||||||||||||||||||||||||||||||||||||||||||||||||||||||||||||||||||

Then, even though I wasn't coaching four sports, I was still consumed with the same level of intensity. I had an insatiable desire to turn my athletes into great performers on the field. I wanted to win games. I wanted to win championships. But I didn't really know why. All the while, I was serving the Lord away from the football field, but I was coaching in a way that didn't always glorify Him. I wasn't even sure if it was possible to do both.

TRAINING TIME

1. At what point in your career did you realize the influence you have on a young person's life?
2. How did that realization impact you?
3. Do you view coaching as a profession or as a calling? Explain.
4. How do you most want to impact the lives of your athletes? Be specific.

PRAYER

Lord, thank You for giving me such an influential platform as a coach. Help me to balance my desire to succeed in my professional life with my desire to fulfill the calling You have placed on my life.

3

COACH BOWDEN

It didn't take long before it was time to take the next big step in my coaching journey. Dana and I were enjoying the early years of marriage. It was still just the two of us. I was coaching high school football. She was teaching second grade. We had also deepened our commitment to First Baptist Church in Plant City. First Baptist was my wife's home church and the place where we were married.

One day after Sunday service, a gentleman named Harold Taylor approached me and struck up a conversation. Howard was president of the First National Bank of Plant City where we got our first loan on a singlewide mobile home. He was also one of the church deacons. Perhaps most importantly to the moment was his status as a "Golden Chief." In other words, Howard was a major Florida State donor and was well connected to the athletic department.

"We have this great Christian coach we've brought in and I'd like for you to meet him," Howard enthusiastically said. "His name is Bobby Bowden."

Football wasn't always great at Florida State in Tallahassee. The running joke back then was that fans should never buy a ticket on the 40-yard line. Instead, they should buy a ticket on the 10-yard line and slide over to the empty seats on the 40. When Coach Bowden arrived in 1976, the program was going through a substantial downturn. In the three years before his arrival, the Seminoles had struggled to a disappointing 4-29 record.

But Coach Bowden was turning things around. The team went 5-6 his first year before experiencing a breakthrough season in 1977. Florida State went 10-2 and won the Tangerine Bowl. It was during that offseason when I stepped into Coach Bowden's office for the first time.

Coach Bowden has always been one of the most gregarious figures in college football. That certainly was the case even during his early years at Florida State. It didn't matter if you were a star recruit, another head coach, a major donor, or the custodian, Coach Bowden treated everyone the same. And when he met someone new, he always made sure there was something about you that he could remember in case he came across your path in the future.

Of course, I didn't know that about Coach Bowden at the time. I was just a young high school coach wandering into a Division 1 head football coach's office and trying not to let the situation overwhelm me.

Any feelings of intimidation quickly melted away. Coach Bowden's firm handshake and big smile always had that effect. Within minutes, it felt as if we were two friends sitting down for a casual conversation about family, football and life. To my surprise, I walked out with an offer to join his staff as a volunteer coach. It was the chance of a lifetime and one I couldn't turn down.

The Second Nudge

My wife and I packed up our belongings and moved to Tallahassee that spring. I was excited about the challenge but still somewhat nervous about the leap from high school to Division 1 college football.

That summer, Coach Bowden hosted an annual event he called "Hideaway," where he and the assistant coaches would get out of town on a retreat. For three days, we lived together, ate together and worked on the entire season package. We mapped out our game plans for offense, defense and special teams.

Towards the end of the retreat, Coach Bowden had one last announcement to make. Every assistant would be required to take on an area of responsibility that was outside of his coaching duties. For instance, one of the coaches would need to serve as a liaison between the football program and the academic advisors, while another might be required to help organize dorm assignments for the athletes.

As Coach Bowden went down the list, I sat quietly in my seat— unsure of what job I could best handle.

"You guys know how important this is to me," Coach Bowden barked. "I need somebody who's gonna do the FCA."

FCA, I thought to myself. *I'm a Christian. I can do that.*

I quickly raised my hand.

"Great, Jeff," Coach Bowden affirmed. "Come by and see me in the office next week and I'll tell you what you need to do."

I didn't really need much explanation—or so I thought. By the time my appointment with Coach Bowden arrived, I had already figured everything out. As far as I knew, FCA was about bringing in a speaker, feeding the players, and having a nice little youth-group type of get-together. I wasn't making a lot of money as a graduate assistant, so I picked Thursday nights after practice as our meeting time because that was steak and shrimp night in the cafeteria. I could bring someone on campus to help with the FCA meeting. That was going to be my wife. The way I saw it, we'd be able to get a great meal at least once a week. That was the depth of my spirituality. My approach to FCA ministry was based on what food we were going to eat!

The following week, despite my big plans, I started to feel intimidated again as I stepped into Coach Bowden's office. I recalled something I had heard about him and how he conducted his business.

According to the other coaches, he truly had an open-door policy. He never closed his door. You could stop by and see him anytime, no matter who you were. But if his door was closed, that was not a good sign. That usually meant he was getting on somebody. And if a *coach* was in there, it probably meant something hadn't worked out and that he and Coach Bowden were about to part ways. You didn't want the door closed.

Coach Bowden stood up and warmly welcomed me with a smile and a handshake. "Jeff! Come on in!"

As I looked for a place to sit, I noticed that Coach Bowden was heading for the door. Before my nerves could react, he gently pulled the handle until the door made a distinct clicking sound.

He just closed the door! I anxiously thought to myself. *He can't fire me. I haven't even started yet!*

Coach Bowden walked back over and pulled a chair around to his side of the desk. "Have a seat, Jeff," he nonchalantly ordered.

He pulled his chair around and pulled it up as close as he could until we faced knee to knee. He leaned in, looked me straight in the eye, and said something I'll never forget.

"The world is gonna evaluate us by that scoreboard."

I glanced out his office window. The stadium scoreboard was perfectly visible from where I sat.

"I know that and you need to know that, and that's okay." Coach Bowden continued. "I want to win and I have to win if I want to stay around here. But I'm gonna tell you how *I'm* gonna evaluate you and how I'm gonna evaluate our program."

Although I wasn't sure what was coming next, I was captivated by his presence and moved by his passionate delivery.

"We get these boys for three, four, maybe five years. When they leave this program, I need to know that their place in heaven is secure.

These kids have *got* to be different. FCA is the vehicle that allows us to share the Gospel with these kids."

A sizeable lump formed in my throat. All of my great plans were crashing down around me. I thought FCA was just a nice little thing to do with the athletes once a week. I saw it as an opportunity to get a free meal. But now, here was Coach Bowden telling me that he's going to evaluate me based on how these young men grew spiritually!

I had never encountered a head coach like this before. It was the first time I'd been told that I was supposed to use my influence as a coach to reach athletes for Christ. As I sat there stunned, I could feel a second nudge from the Holy Spirit. He was reminding me again that there is great power in this thing called coaching.

Caught in the Bright Lights

Over the next three years, Florida State enjoyed a meteoric rise to national prominence. The winning mesmerized me and everyone else I knew. Grown men and women—just like the ones I sat next to in church on Sunday—who were prim and proper, coat-and-tie folks would show up at Doak Campbell Stadium with war paint on their faces and feathers in their hats.

The sudden obsession with Seminole football revealed a universal need that so many of us have. We have a drive to compete. But since most of us never reach competition level, we transfer that energy into our manic support of a sports team. We watch a bunch of 18- to 22-year-old kids run around on a 120-yard field covered in various team colors by which we somehow identify ourselves. Yet not one of us has actually competed! Not one of us has played a single down! We haven't made a catch, made a tackle or scored a touchdown!

At the time, I didn't know it, but I was starting to walk on a path that was detrimental to my spirit. Pride had started to creep in and I started to have a feeling of self-importance. It was getting easier and easier to get caught up in the bright lights of big-time college football. I wasn't just a coach; I was a fan of the game. It was intoxicating and it began to have a negative impact on the way I approached my job.

In my second year at Florida State, I was asked to assist in the passing game and to work specifically with the tight ends. The tight ends were a pivotal part of our offense. We often rotated plays through that position. Having a fairly important responsibility, I wanted desperately to impress the other coaches and show them that I could get the job done.

Midway through the season, we were ranked number 11 after a 5-1 start. Our only loss was a 10-9 slugfest against number 9-ranked Miami that was played in the Orange Bowl. But now we were preparing for a home game against number 4-ranked Pitt. The Panthers were undefeated and boasted one of the most talented teams in the country. Future NFL Hall of Fame quarterback Dan Marino was a sophomore at Pitt that season. Other star players included offensive tackle Mark May (now an ESPN analyst) and future NFL Hall of Fame players Russ Grimm and Rickey Jackson.

But from my perspective, the biggest challenge would come from one of the most dominant outside linebackers in the game. Hugh Green would finish his career as a three-time All-American and would go on to have a long All-Pro NFL career as a first-round draft pick. His stellar career also landed him a spot in the College Football Hall of Fame.

Green was unstoppable. He lined up in multiple positions and would blitz with no rhyme or reason. As we reviewed the film, our offensive coordinator, George Henshaw, emphasized the importance of our tight ends' blocking the C gap. Green was noted for lining up inside and then shooting into the C gap between the tight end and the tackle. All week long, I diligently worked with our tight ends on blocking down and making sure we covered the C gap on plays that required pass protection.

On game day, the stadium was filled with over 55,000 fans. We won the toss and elected to receive the opening kickoff. Pitt kicked the ball to our return guy who botched the catch and picked it up before being tackled inside our own 10-yard line. Even with the bad field position, Coach Bowden called for a long play action pass as he typically did on the first play of the game.

The tight end's job was to step down and make sure that nobody got into the C gap before he would release to the flat as a secondary receiver. When the ball was snapped, our tight end saw Green lined up on the outside. Green took a jab step as if to indicate he was going to run to the flat. Instead of stepping down into the C gap, the tight end believed he was okay to release his spot and make himself available for a pass.

But after the jab step, Green blitzed inside the tight end and took a clear path to our quarterback. Green made the tackle in the end zone and scored a safety. Just one play into the game and we were down 2-0.

Dead silence. That's all I could hear on my headset. No one said a word, but I could feel Coach Bowden's and Coach Henshaw's eyes looking at me. Here I was, a young coach who was trying to make a great impression and I had failed. It was a simple assignment that we had worked on all week.

What went wrong?

I didn't understand it at the time, but my faulty approach became crystal clear much later in my journey to becoming a 3D Coach. Our team wasn't noted for having great blocking tight ends, although we had done a reasonably good job thus far in the season. That week, however, I coached them differently than before:

1. I continually showed our tight ends film of them missing blocking assignments in previous games.
2. I showed them film of Hugh Green blitzing and destroying offensive lines.
3. During practice, I voiced my displeasure (rather loudly) every time one of the tight ends showed signs of poor blocking techniques.

I will never forget that episode. I had to ask myself some tough, introspective questions:

- *Why was I coaching that way?*
- *Why was it so hard to praise the positive things?*
- *Why was it so easy to point out the mistakes?*

Regardless of where I was coaching, I could always figure out practical issues with an athlete or a team. I had no problem teaching my players the fundamentals of the game. If there were things I didn't know, I would go to a clinic or pick up a book to find the answers.

But what about situations like the one I faced with those tight ends? How could I have taught them all the *right* things and still have come away with a poor result? I really loved coaching, but for some reason that I couldn't fully explain there was always an underlying sense of frustration. Even during those incredible years at Florida State, I was still unfulfilled as a coach.

The Transformational Coach

Bobby Bowden wasn't the most knowledgeable man to coach college football. Don't get me wrong. He knew the game, but not at some super-elevated level. His ability to break down *X*s and *O*s wasn't why he was so successful. Coach Bowden was great because he had an uncanny ability to connect with young athletes even during his later years at Florida State where he retired at the age of 80.

||||||||||||||||||||||||||||||||||||||||||||||||||||||||||||||||||||||||||||||||||||||||||||||||

To this day, Coach Bowden's greatest legacy was his ability to understand the mindsets of his players and then establish lasting relationships with those players, their parents and his fellow coaches.

||||||||||||||||||||||||||||||||||||||||||||||||||||||||||||||||||||||||||||||||||||||||||||||||

There are many stories to be told about how Coach Bowden's influence was bigger than the game. One that comes to mind took place a few years after I had left Florida State.

Sammie Smith was a highly recruited high school running back out of Apopka, Florida. Coach Bowden convinced this teenager from a poverty-stricken background to play at Florida State. After a successful college career, Sammie was drafted in the first round of the 1989 NFL Draft with the ninth overall pick. He spent four seasons in Miami and Denver before injuries prematurely ended his career.

Sammie made millions of dollars playing in the league but lost it all. Desperate to make ends meet, he turned to the streets where he sold cocaine. Sammie was arrested and sent to the federal penitentiary for seven years. While incarcerated, he spent a lot of his time reminiscing about his days at Florida State. He harkened back to the lessons he had learned from Coach Bowden.

When Sammie came up for parole, he felt good about his chances of an early release. But no one was there to speak on his behalf. He was estranged from his wife and three daughters. His family was nowhere to be found. As he went to appear in front of the judge, the back doors suddenly flung open. Coach Bowden had showed up to take the stand.

"Let me tell you about the Sammie Smith I know," he said to the judge. "He was always a great team player. Yeah, he made a mistake. But I believe he's ready to move on and become a productive citizen of Florida again!"

Sammie breaks down every time he tells this story. He is now serving as an FCA Area Representative in central Florida.

A transactional coach wouldn't have cared about Sammie's plight. A transactional coach would have said, "That was 12 years ago! Sammie Smith isn't going to help me win another football game!"

But a relational coach is different. A relational coach gets involved in an athlete's life. A relational coach sees the big picture and sees young people as individuals, not just as numbers on a jersey or as positions on a depth chart. That's what made Coach Bowden special. I didn't know it at the time, but I was observing firsthand what a 3D Coach looks like. I see it now. I didn't see it then.

I should have been content at Florida State. My story should have stopped there. I was on a Division 1 campus. I had coached in two Orange Bowls. I was in charge of an important recruiting area. Instead, I found myself constantly looking for something more.

TRAINING TIME

1. Who has been the most influential person or mentor thus far in your coaching career, and why?
2. Can you describe a time when you felt like you let someone down as a coach? Why do you think you felt that way?

3. What would you say are the major differences between a relational coach and a transactional coach? What kinds of results can each expect?
4. In what ways, as Coach Bowden asserts, do you think athletes should be different when they leave your program?

PRAYER

Lord, help me take my eyes off the scoreboard and keep them fixed on the big picture. Give me the strength to do my job with excellence while tending to the spiritual needs of my athletes.

4

THE ALLURE OF THE
NEXT LEVEL

While I should have been happy at Florida State, I instead found myself contending with something that seems to plague a lot of coaches. I like to call it "the allure of the next level." We begin to fill ourselves up with the things of this world. At the same time, we try to balance this thing called Christianity. Over time, the seesaw starts tilting more heavily towards the things of the world, and before we know it, our priorities are turned completely upside down.

I was so confused at the time. I loved coaching, but it wasn't filling me up. It didn't matter what the level—junior varsity, varsity or college—I couldn't find fulfillment within the profession that meant so much to me.

Maybe I should do something spiritual.

It was a strange thought, but at the time it seemed logically sound. I left Florida State and went to work for FCA. The organization was expanding nationally and even internationally. It was an exciting time to be involved with sports ministry. What I didn't understand was that my mission field, my calling, was right in front of me all along. I succumbed to a desire for something more.

For the next three years, I served as the North Florida/South Georgia Area Director of FCA. I hauled college athletes, mostly from Florida State, around to different schools, churches and youth groups so they could share their testimonies. There was nothing wrong with that. In fact, it was an awesome thing. But that wasn't what I was called to do. What I ultimately learned was that I wasn't a very good FCA staff person. I was essentially a tour guide, a liaison of sorts.

I finally realized that I needed to get back into coaching, but by then I'd lost my place. Eventually I did what many coaches do. I took what seemed to be the next logical step in my professional journey and got into athletic administration. I took a job as Director of Athletics and Activities for the Leon County School Board in Tallahassee, where I was charged with creating and implementing job descriptions for 200 coaches and athletic directors. This also included developing booster bylaws, implementing sweeping changes in legislation, such as Title IX directives, supervising centralized funding and purchasing, and overseeing ethical directives concerning coach, parent and athlete behavior.

|||||||||||||||||||||||||||||||||||||||||||||||||||||||||||||||||||||||||||||||||||||||||||||||||||||

I was making more money and I had more people listening to me, but I was still frustrated. I missed coaching.

|||||||||||||||||||||||||||||||||||||||||||||||||||||||||||||||||||||||||||||||||||||||||||||||||||||

All the while, my family started to grow. During my time in Tallahassee, Dana and I welcomed our four sons into the world—Bo, Cameron, and our twins, Matt and Mark. With the increased responsibility of parenthood, I continued to look for the next step in my professional journey.

A Date with Disney

The next opportunity came within the realm of sports tourism working for the Tallahassee Area Sports Council. From there, my reputation grew until eventually the Florida Governor's Council on Physical Fitness and Sports approached me about helping develop sports tourism within the state. I eventually started my own consulting company that landed a contract with the Walt Disney Company and their initiative for developing the Wide World of Sports complex in Orlando (now called the ESPN Wide World of Sports).

Tallahassee had been a secure environment for our family. My wife loved her teaching job and my kids loved their schools. We were part of a wonderful church and community. I had all of the checkpoints that a man is supposed to have throughout his adult years as a husband and father. But here I was, packing up the family and moving on to the next big thing.

One of my first jobs was recruiting teams to train in Florida prior to the Olympic Games in Atlanta. That required quite a bit of world travel. It was a strange turn of events for someone who loved coaching. But that hadn't been enough. It hadn't been enough at the high school level. It hadn't been enough at Florida State. Sports ministry with FCA wasn't enough either. It was the same thing in athletic administration. The power, the money and the prestige were never enough. Now the world I sought was literally the world!

||||||||||||||||||||||||||||||||||||||||||||||||||||||||||||||||||||||||||||||||||||||||||||||||||||||||

The allure of the next level keeps us looking
for the next big thing.

||||||||||||||||||||||||||||||||||||||||||||||||||||||||||||||||||||||||||||||||||||||||||||||||||||||||

As my self-worth continued to become overinflated, I told those around me (and myself) that I was doing it for all the right reasons. I was traveling the globe and was gone for long stretches at a time to make more money and to better provide for my family. But deep inside, I was filling up with pride. Bigger was better. It was the same as what we see in today's coaching world.

In the years following the Atlanta Olympics, sports tourism in central Florida continued to flourish and I was right in the middle of it all. This led to a major contract between the British Olympic Association and the state of Florida. British Olympians would come to central Florida to train in the warm weather. Disney could then promote that Olympic athletes were training in their complex. It was one big marketing ploy and I was the lynch pin. I was supposed to make it all happen.

I'll never forget the night before the contract was about to be signed. We were going to have a press conference at Wembley Stadium. Members of the Royal Family were scheduled to attend. The president of Walt Disney had flown to London for the event. Several years of work had led me to this point. I had put all of my eggs into this basket. I was the man!

During the negotiations, the International Olympic Committee showed concern over the use of the Olympic rings. The IOC owns the rings but every country has the right to use them within their country. Different nations have different Olympic logos that are allowed. The United States, for example, has "USA" and the five rings. Great Britain has a picture of a lion (their national symbol) and the five rings.

I knew about these territorial restrictions and so did Disney. But the IOC was concerned that Disney might violate the use of the rings within the United States. Disney had no intention of doing so. They were strictly going to use the rings within Great Britain. Otherwise, everything seemed to be in order.

That's when I got a phone call that would dramatically change my life. One of the Disney officials and a close friend of mine asked to meet with me.

"Jeff, we just got word that the contract is going to be voided," he somberly reported. "Jeff, you realize that this is how we've been able to pay you."

"Yeah, I know," I replied.

"Jeff," he repeated. "That's how we've been able to pay you."

And it hit me. I was 40 years old. I was across the ocean. And I'd just lost my job.

Sitting in the back of a pub, tears flowed from my eyes. A flood of emotions and thoughts crashed inside my head. As I eventually gained my composure, I realized I needed to call Dana. There was a six-hour time difference between London and Orlando. It was still afternoon back home. After I explained the situation, she spoke these sobering words. "Listen, Jeff. You come on home. You're not the man I married. You're not the man I married."

I knew I wasn't the man she married. I had gotten caught up in the allure of the next level. I was seeking man's approval. I wanted the world's applause.

IIIIIIIIIIIIIIIIIIIIIIIIIIIIIIIIIIIIIIIIIIIIIIIIIIIIIIIIIIIIIIIIIIIIIIIIIIIIIIIIIIIIIIIIIIIIIIIIIIIIIIIIIII

When what you do becomes who you are, and then
you lose what you do, you find out who you really are.

IIIIIIIIIIIIIIIIIIIIIIIIIIIIIIIIIIIIIIIIIIIIIIIIIIIIIIIIIIIIIIIIIIIIIIIIIIIIIIIIIIIIIIIIIIIIIIIIIIIIIIIIIII

I was pretty empty. I hadn't been a very good husband. My wife had been back home with the four boys while I was traveling the world pretending that I was doing it all for them, but I was really doing it all for me. I began asking myself some very difficult questions:

- *What is this all about?*
- *What have I been chasing?*

• *Why am I not at peace?*

I had read so many Scriptures that talk about being content in Christ, yet I had no contentment. I had no peace. I was constantly restless. I was never satisfied. It was always about the next step. I had put my wife on the backburner of my life and I was about to lose her.

As I headed home, I was completely broken. My emotional state was the hardest place to be, but looking back, it was the place I needed to be the most.

TRAINING TIME

1. Why did you originally get into coaching?
2. Have your reasons for coaching changed over time or have they stayed the same? If they have changed, how so?
3. What are your career goals as they pertain to promotions, dream jobs, and so on?
4. Do you ever find yourself getting professionally restless? If so, what do you think is the reason for that restlessness?
5. What are some things that might help you find contentment in your current position?

PRAYER

Lord, help me to be content with where I've been placed. Line up my goals with Your perfect will for my life, and give me patience as I continue down this path.

5

BROKEN

As I flew back home to Florida, there was a nagging question for which I had no satisfactory answer.

How did I get here?

Since accepting Christ at the age of 12, I had never turned my back on the Lord. I felt that I had faithfully served Him. But here I was, sitting on a plane, devastated—almost as if my life had ended—because some big contract had fallen through.

Within days of losing the contract with the British Olympic Association, I received a call from a local principal who was preparing to open a new high school in the area where I lived. He knew my history as a coach and recruiter and thought I would have good insight on possible candidates for their head football coaching position. Then he asked me an interesting question.

"Jeff, do you have time to chair the committee and help us pick a coach?"

Do I have time? I thought to myself. I'll never forget those words. Here's how I viewed time. I *owned* time. Time was something I did. I could show you my calendar and it was nailed to the minute. I always knew what I was doing and how I was doing it. I could out-recruit you, out-hustle you and out-work you. No matter where I was employed, I would be judged by how much I did in this thing called time. But now, for the first time in almost 20 years, I didn't own time anymore. What I did—this career by which I'd identified myself—was no longer there. My answer was immediately clear.

"Yes, sir," I meekly replied. "I have time."

The Third Nudge

The principal gave me a box full of applications—probably close to 90—and I began thumbing through them. I was surprised to come across the name of a coach I had met years earlier in my recruiting and administrative work.

Here is what I knew about him: He was in his early 50s. He had won a bunch of games, two state championships even, but I would not want my dog to play for him. He seemed angry and ruthless when he coached his athletes. They performed well, but it was done in a way that didn't seem healthy.

Clermont East Ridge, as the new school was going to be called, just happened to be in our neighborhood. Cameron, my second son, was going to be playing football there. Whoever was hired would be *my* son's coach. So I thought to myself, *This guy isn't getting the job.* I didn't want that kind of coach influencing my kid. However, when you are broken and humbled, God will speak to you—and He did. It was as clear as the words you are reading in this book today.

Call him.

Looking back, I now realize this was the third distinct nudge from the Holy Spirit. It's so much easier to see these things years after God's plan has been fully revealed. I hadn't talked to this coach in several years. When he answered the phone, we exchanged pleasantries and typical guy talk. I heard a different voice than the one I remembered from before. Then I finally cut to the chase.

"Coach, I noticed you applied for this job and I'm on the committee to select candidates. What's going on?"

"I got out of coaching two years ago," he told me.

This guy's applying for a job and he's not even coaching anymore? I thought to myself. *That doesn't make a bit of sense.*

As we continued to talk, he explained to me that during all the winning (and because he was so driven to win), his wife had left him and his two sons had nearly disowned him. On a personal level, he had hit rock bottom and in the process had made some of the same discoveries I had made along my journey.

"There's got to be more," he told me, echoing some of the same words I'd been contemplating. "I'm asking myself the tougher questions. What is it all about?"

Then he asked if we could meet.

"Coach, I don't know," I responded. "I've never hired a public high school coach. I'm just on a committee."

"I don't want to talk about football," he quickly retorted. "I want to talk about more important things."

That's when I knew I had to meet with him. So on a Saturday in February, we met at a Burger King for breakfast. He had driven an hour south and I had driven an hour north. When I walked in, I saw a bald-headed coach in the back corner with a Bible, a sausage biscuit and a coffee. I knew immediately there was something different about Bud O'Hara.

For the next three or four hours, two *broken* coaches talked about what it might look like to coach the *right way*. Could you really coach according to biblical standards and still be good? It was the greatest coaching conversation I'd ever had. I've been to countless football clinics and heard some of the greatest coaches speak. But in the back of that Burger King on a Saturday morning, I was deeply moved when he held his Bible up and said, "If I ever get a head coaching job again, I want to do it right."

Bud went through the interview process and eventually made the short list. As we narrowed it down to the final two candidates, our committee came together to decide who should be hired. The group included a couple of players, a couple of parents and key members of the school administration. I'll never forget how adamant the players and parents were in their desire to hire Bud. They saw something in him that transcended his impeccable coaching ability.

Bud was ready to take a renewed mindset into a new job and he wanted *me* to be his offensive coordinator. He ended up getting the job and I joined him for a journey that would last about 10 years and continues today. It was during that time that we both found peace and contentment. Sure, we won a bunch of games and some district championships. We also helped send some kids to college. But it was so much greater than that because we had discovered a better way to do the thing we loved to do.

As Bud once told me years later, "You can do it the right way and have joy and peace, or you can do it the old way and be miserable." Everything we did was about showing those kids the love of Christ. When you do that, the difference is night and day.

Coaching in a Broken Culture

During my time coaching with Bud, I got more serious about finishing the doctorate work I had started while working as an athletic director. But this time, I had a greater purpose. I wanted to really understand the role of the coach in our culture today. I returned to Florida State and found Dr. Beverly Yerg, a person in the department who was also a strong believer. I told her that I wanted to study what makes a great coach in our culture today. Could you really be great on the field and balance your spiritual life? Can they really work hand in hand?

"Let's find out," Dr. Bev said.

One of the first things I discovered was also one of the most obvious. A lot has changed since my junior high and high school playing days. Coaches from that era didn't have to worry about coaching beyond the first dimension. The role of the coach was simply dealing with athletics. That's mostly because young athletes were more likely to get the emotional and spiritual support from home.

There used to be something called "blind obedience." I grew up in the last era of blind obedience. Many people call that era the "Greatest Generation." That generation fought in World War II and did things for the betterment of the country. They didn't ask why. They just did it.

When I played, it was easier to coach. We didn't talk about three dimensions. Everything could be handled in the first dimension.

Do what I say. If you mess up, I'll call your parents and they'll fix it.

One call and the parents handled it. There was a stronger traditional home life during that time. Most children had a mother and a father, and a respect for authority. Whatever parents, police officers, teachers, pastors or coaches said to do, you did it; just like the time when my dad demanded that I keep my commitment to the football team when I wanted to quit.

After World War II, our nation began to experience great material affluence. And suddenly, there was never enough. Before long, the generations that practiced blind obedience were gone and were replaced by the entitlement generation. That generation makes up the kids we coach today.

And that's not the only way our culture is broken. The statistics bear out this truth. This country's divorce rate is over 50% while the second-time divorce rate is roughly 70%. Even more telling is the fact that 72% of this nation's kids don't have both biological parents at home. Think about it. Three out of every four children have heard at least one biological parent say these devastating words: "I quit."

This is by no means an indictment against divorce. There are incredible single moms out there doing a wonderful job raising their kids alone. And there are loving stepparents who bridge the gap during difficult transitions within a blended family unit. But let's be honest in our assessment of how divorce and the increase of single-parent households are drastically changing the dynamics for today's coaches. Think for a moment about what happens when you call a parent today. Chances are you're going to connect with one of the two following types:

1. *The non-involved parent*: This parent shows little interest in what their child is doing at school or perhaps is too busy due to financial, marital or emotional stress. Oftentimes, these parents enforce few if any boundaries for their children. Half the time, they don't even know what their child is doing. Because of that, the child lacks a firm sense of commitment and struggles with basic moral issues. And if parents aren't committed to their own families, how can we expect a kid to stay committed just for the greater good of a sports team?

2. *The hyper-involved parent*: This parent has bought into the cultural lie that sports can fix the problems within their children's lives. They struggle to deal with their children's behavioral, emotional or moral problems and therefore pass that responsibility along to the coach. In other instances, the hyper-involved parent sees sports as a catchall opportunity for their child to be successful in life. Sports are viewed merely as a means to an end. In other words, sports will help their child get a scholarship and have a better chance at long-term professional and financial security.

It's the hyper-involved parent that somehow manages to be at every afternoon practice. You wonder, *Do these guys have jobs?* How they get off work every day to show up for their kid's practices is a mystery. Sadly, they are often not there to show support as much as they are there to keep an eye on the coaches or feel good about themselves based on their child's performance.

So here we are in this broken culture. The concept of blind obedience is a thing of the past. Authority is no longer respected as it was two or three generations ago. Instead, coaches are seeing the brokenness within families negatively impacting their athletes' ability to perform in practice and during competition.

Our broken culture is further complicated when you throw sports into the mix. That's why I don't get mad at the parents anymore. They just want their kid to be on the all-star team. They just want something great to happen for their kid. When the kid performs well, the parents feel better about themselves.

The problem is that our society no longer knows what greatness is. We have an identity crisis. We only know how to define it with material, athletic or academic success. Sports are one of the things that at least give us a way to measure success:

- *My kid scored 10 touchdowns!*
- *My kid batted .425!*
- *My kid got a scholarship offer from a Division 1 school!*

That's what coaches are dealing with today. Coaches must navigate the perilous waters of lack of parental involvement and the reality of unrealistic expectations—both of which are wrapped up in this broken sports culture that daily proclaims the virtues of winning. Now is the most difficult time to be a coach, but it *can* be the most rewarding.

Stuck in the First Dimension

First of all, let's make sure to get this important fact out of the way. The first dimension is a vital part of the coaching experience. It's within that realm that we find the keys to successful athlete development—basic elements such as strength, power, speed, quickness, cardio, technique, repetition and tactics. It is the physicality of sport, and sport *is* physical!

If we don't understand the basic principles of our sport and work to become excellent as teachers of those principles, then we won't be in the coaching profession for very long. The Bible calls us to be excellent, no matter what we do in life. Consider these words written by the apostle Paul:

> Whatever you do, work at it with all your heart, as working for the Lord, not for human masters, since you know that you will receive an inheritance from the Lord as a reward. It is the Lord Christ you are serving (Col. 3:23-24).

In other words, God expects us to give our best with the gifts and talents that He has given us. It should be our way of thanking Him for those opportunities and giving the glory back to Him. When we talk about coaching beyond the first dimension, we're not diminishing the importance of teaching fundamentals or de-emphasizing the need for physical training. On the contrary, we fully acknowledge and affirm the coaches' requirement to do their absolute best to instruct athletes at the foundational level.

And here's another interesting thing about the first dimension. Every miracle Jesus did started with a physical need. Why did He take a few fish and a few loaves to feed thousands? It's simple. People had been there all day and were hungry! If you don't take care of things in the first dimension (the physical), then you can't jump to the second dimension (the relational) or the third dimension (the spiritual). That's what makes His miracles so incredible. He could have turned the grass blue, but that wouldn't have met the people's needs.

There are some major problems that can occur when we get stuck in the first dimension and fail to address matters of the heart. Meeting the physical needs bears little weight if we stop there. Do any of these problems sound familiar?

- Athletes become unmotivated in practice and during competition, especially when the season does not meet expectations.
- Athletes pull back in big game situations; they do not play to their full potential when the lights go on.
- Emotions of parents and players are all over the place. They are disgruntled, disenchanted and either over-involved or not involved at all.
- Athletes and parents are selfish and have a "what's in it for me" mentality.

The likelihood is that we have *all* faced these problems, and if you've been in the coaching profession for very long, these problems have become more frequent and more intense. If you're like me, you also have tried to fix these problems with first-dimension solutions, such as physical punishment (pushups, laps, etc.) or other disciplinary methods (loss of playing time, suspension from team, etc.).

Unfortunately, it's not that simple anymore. It has become nearly impossible to fix second-dimension problems (matters of the heart) in the first dimension. As we move forward, we'll look at these issues more closely and discern some of the second-dimension solutions that will revolutionize and revitalize your life as a coach.

Getting stuck in the first dimension can have repercussions that go well beyond the scope of your athletic program. It seems that more and more, coaches are having marital and family problems because of this fixation on the performance-based culture of winning. So many coaches cannot contrast the winning mentality of a team and the loving mentality of a spouse and parent. First-dimension coaching always separates the two while 3Dimensional Coaching unites the two.

Take for instance, the story of a good friend of mine who won five collegiate national championships but lost his wife in the midst of the winning. Today, as a 3D Coach, he understands that he did not have to separate his two loves—coaching and being a husband.

I have seen him demonstrate this at major coaching conventions when he places five national championship rings on the podium and then reaches into his pocket and pulls out his wedding ring and says these powerful words:

"I would give up all five of these [pointing to the championship rings] if I could have this one back [pointing to his wedding ring]."

This coach didn't learn about 3Dimensional Coaching in time to save his marriage, but I can happily report that he has remarried and found the balance between having a deep and loving relationship while still coaching with greatness. It can be done!

For that coach, losing his first marriage was the tragic result of a man succumbing to the pressures within a broken sports culture. His loss served as a humbling wake-up call.

In my life, losing the contract with the British Olympic Association shook me to the core. As it turns out, that so-called failure ended up being the greatest part of my career. Until that point, I had wanted both the things of this world and the Lord. I had clearly forgotten the words that Jesus wrote in Matthew 16:26:

And what do you benefit if you gain the whole world but lose your own soul? Is anything worth more than your soul? (*NLT*).

When my heart was turned back to God's perfect will for my life, only then was I able to find true peace and contentment. It took a hard collision between my competing worlds before I could realize that His blessings were wrapped up in a relationship with Him, not in the progression of my career. Now I was ready to understand what it truly meant to become a 3D Coach.

TRAINING TIME

1. What are some ways that today's broken culture has negatively impacted your ability to be effective as a coach?
2. Which is more difficult for you to deal with as a coach: the non-involved parent or the hyper-involved parent? Explain.
3. How do you define excellence? What are some ways you try to get excellence out of your athletes?
4. Reread Colossians 3:23-24. How does this passage relate to excellence? Does it challenge or reaffirm what you believe to be the purpose behind striving for excellence? Why?

PRAYER

Lord, guide my steps as I navigate through a broken culture that threatens to negatively impact me and the athletes that I coach. Give me the wisdom to understand the true meaning of excellence and the strength to do my best as I challenge my athletes to fulfill their potential.

6

KNOWING YOUR TURF

As I took a closer look at the profession I loved so much, the broken culture (and its impact on sports) became crystal clear. I knew in my heart that there had to be a practical solution to the problems I had faced during my early days as a coach.

In my previous experiences, I had mostly coached in the first dimension. I had relied solely on the physical aspects of coaching and failed to intentionally meet the emotional and spiritual needs of my players. Because of that, I found myself basing my self-worth on how the kids performed and the success or failure of my teams.

Through intensive study, I began to have a better understanding of relational, purpose-driven leadership that I now refer to as 3Dimensional Coaching. It was a revelation of principles that go much deeper than the physicality of sports.

What I learned is that holistic coaching is done in three dimensions:

- First Dimension = Body (Physical)
- Second Dimension = Mind (Emotional)
- Third Dimension = Spirit (Spiritual)

I wish someone had come alongside me when I was 23 and walked me through this process. What I studied in my doctoral program was the role and impact of the coach in American culture. What I discovered through research has been one of the most interesting journeys I have ever experienced. Coaches today who coach in three dimensions are the ones with great balance: great on the field, great in the athlete's mindset, and great in understanding their own journey. The outflow is that the kids play great and with great purpose.

You see, when what you do becomes who you are and what you do is taken away from you, you find out who you really are; and I was not much. Now I began to put the pieces together: Purpose and mission *must* go hand in hand.

Once I made this important self-discovery, I finally found peace and contentment as a coach. I immediately felt a strong desire in my heart to help other coaches experience that same revolution. Here I was at 40 doing what I was called to do when I was 20—coaching the way God had planned for me to coach. Hence, 3Dimensional Coaching was birthed.

What Is 3Dimensional Coaching?

As we discussed briefly in the last chapter, there are three realms within which coaching should take place. *The First Dimension* is the foundational aspect of sports. It is based in the physical realm. This is where we teach fundamentals and train the body for specific tasks.

It doesn't matter what sport you coach. Sport is physical. You have to jump. You have to run. You have to hit. You have to catch. You have to slide. Fundamentals are sport specific. If you're not good at coaching these things in the first dimension, then you won't last very long in the profession.

Tactics are also a very important part of first-dimension coaching. For instance, in football, there has been a shift by many teams to the 3-5 defense in an effort to combat the pervasive popularity of the spread offense. No matter what the sport, coaches who have trouble adjusting to schematic changes will struggle to maintain their positions.

But first-dimension problems are teachable and measurable, and we have vast resources at our disposal to help identify and fix those areas of concern. Today, coaches labor most intensely when outside forces beyond their control enter the picture and threaten to downgrade individual and team performance. These are what we define as "second-dimension" problems.

The Second Dimension is defined by what takes place in the athlete's mind and how that connects to physical performance. Some people call this psychology. But when it comes to sports, I prefer to use the word "dualism," which simply means that the mind and the body are united. If the mind and body work as separate entities, then both underperform. But when they work in concert, performance increases.

There are eight major areas impacted by the dualism between the body and the mind, but for the purpose of this presentation, we are going to focus on what we believe are the four most important keys to capturing the athlete's heart: (1) motivation, (2) confidence, (3) emotions and (4) team cohesion. Let's take a quick look at each of these components.

1. Motivation

Motivation is the inclination to pursue and persist in the journey towards a desired outcome.

Are you tired of trying to motivate kids today? What most of us want from players are two things: great attitude and great effort. How much more fun and how much easier would it be if every day that you went to practice, every single kid brought great attitude and great effort? That would make it very fun and very easy.

The problem is that the kids have changed. They always want more. No matter what, it's never enough. How many of you are dealing with parents who think their kids are better than they really are? They think little Jimmy will get a scholarship. They think Sally should play shortstop. Tom should have been the quarterback. It's never enough.

Now, go to a little league game. The minivan door opens up. Mom and Dad get out of the vehicle and are followed by their little athlete. He's wearing a $50 fitted hat, carrying a $350 Easton bat, and has a pair of $100 Oakley sunglasses turned backward on his baseball hat. The kid is 10 years old and he's wearing $500 worth of stuff!

We've bought into a lie—the lie that says in order to motivate athletes, we need to give them more stuff. In my early years as a coach, my lack of understanding blocked me from moving to the next level.

There's an old saying: People don't care how much you know, until they know how much you care. I don't like clichés, but it comes down to this: 3D Coaches capture the hearts and minds of the players, and that's when true motivation takes place.

2. Confidence

Confidence is an individual's belief that he or she has the necessary skills to produce a desired outcome. The skill is based in the first dimension. It's a movement pattern. Belief jumps into the mental component. The athlete needs to believe that he or she can perform a certain physical skill.

When an athlete loses confidence, he or she hasn't lost the ability to perform the skill, but only the belief. Their mind no longer thinks they can do it. Something breaks in a kid's life, and they suddenly can't perform. A first-dimensional approach is to simply get better at the skill, keep working on it, and hope they get it. In reality, belief needs to be elevated.

3. Emotions

Emotions are the subjective and conscious responses to performance that physiologically, psychologically and/or behaviorally influence an individual's ability to perform sports-related functions.

This is where a passion for sport becomes evident. Why are we buying $500 in gear? Why are sports the number one discretionary activity in our country? It's because we are emotionally tied to the experiences that sports bring to our lives.

Between 30 and 53 million kids in our country have played or play sports during their adolescence. But sports are not required. And once a child gets involved in sports, parents become eager to enter the team culture. We call it the Silo effect. If an athlete is good at a particular sport, that athlete needs to be playing it year round. Baseball teams play in spring leagues, travel to tournaments during the summer and then play in a fall league. Indoor workouts are the norm throughout the winter. It is no longer uncommon for pre-teen youth to play 150 games a year.

Is it right? I don't know. But there's no doubt that sports generate a lot of passion, and passion is an emotion. Emotions can be helpful or detrimental. If some emotions help athletes become better, then coaches need to cultivate those. If emotions are harmful, then those should be downplayed and many times eliminated.

4. Team Cohesion

Team cohesion is the physical and emotional unification of a group of individuals in pursuit of a singular goal.

How do you make a group of players into a team when it's all about me? This nation has now ushered in a second generation of entitlement. Entitlement means I'm owed something. If I do it, I better get something out of it. But team cohesion takes place when your athletes move away from the "it's all about me" mindset to the "we not me" concept.

As you begin to intentionally focus on each of these vital second-dimension issues, you will be amazed at the difference in your athletes, your peers and, perhaps most importantly, yourself. And while coaching in the second dimension is very rewarding, it will fall short if you don't push further into what we call the third dimension.

The Third Dimension

The third dimension is the place in which the highest level of coaching takes place. It is defined by the connection between body, mind and spirit—*holism*. This is when you as a coach are on a spiritual journey that leads to internal transformation. But you can't get there until you realize that you have been placed wherever you are for a reason. You have been entrusted with the lives of young people—and you have great influence.

The third dimension touches on some personal issues that reside deep in our souls—areas such as:

Character
Identity
Purpose
Self-worth
Significance
Value

As you begin to experience transformation, you will then be able to lead your athletes to that same place of discovery. But it's important to remember that you can't be a tour guide to a land where you've never been. You must first go on this journey.

And perhaps the most important thing you need to know before moving forward in this process is that there will be obstacles along the way. If you want to discover what sport was meant to be, you're going to have to go around the values of today's sports culture. It won't be easy. There will be others around you who will resist traveling with you on this journey. 3Dimensional Coaching is by its very nature countercultural, yet it is more fulfilling than anything the current sports model could ever offer.

Why 3Dimensional Coaching?

By now, it should be pretty clear *why* 3D Coaching is so vital in today's society. But let's go ahead and address the question that many of you are already thinking: "Can we still be good if I coach in all three dimensions?"

The answer to that question is unequivocally yes!

Does it mean that you will win every game and collect every championship trophy? Realistically, that will never be the case with any program. But here's what you can expect out of athletes who are led by 3D Coaches:

1. *They will learn skills more quickly; they are more focused.* Today's athletes are bombarded with distractions. It used to drive me nuts when my players couldn't concentrate. That was when I coached solely in the first dimension. What I've found, however, is that 3D Coaches don't have problems with attention because their athletes have bought into something more meaningful and they become more acutely focused.

2. *They have higher fitness compliance; they work harder.* Training in the first dimension will only take an athlete so far

before he or she peaks out. But a 3D Coach can motivate athletes to work harder and push through physical and emotional walls that stand in the way. I saw this firsth and with my son Cameron. While playing under a first-dimension coach, he constantly struggled with his work-outs. But when he started playing under a 3D Coach, he never missed a day in the weight room—even when that meant being there at 6 AM!

3. *They need shorter rehabilitation; they recover from injury quicker.* An injured or banged up athlete often deals with negative emotions such as discouragement, frustration, anger, fear and doubt. But a 3D Coach can encourage that athlete to focus on positive emotions that will often lead to quicker recovery times.

4. *They are more adaptable to new conditions; they play just as well on the road as they do at home.* When athletes are coached in the first dimension, a change in the environment (e.g., playing on another team's field) can easily shake their confidence due to a fear of failure. But 3D Coaches produce athletes who are aren't as worried about factors that are out of their control. Sometimes, they even play better on the road!

5. *They have the freedom to be creative; they are "gamers."* Very much like adaptability, athletes who are coached through fear will resist the opportunity to try new skills. So many athletes never play to their full potential when the lights go on for fear of one thing: failure. But athletes who experience 3Dimensional Coaching don't fear failure. Instead, they relish the opportunity to broaden their horizons.

6. *They learn life lessons better through the coach-athlete relationship.* It's a simple truth. First-dimension coaches struggle

to relate greater life principles to their athletes because so much emphasis is placed on performance and temporal rewards. But 3D Coaches lead in a way that places sports within the greater context of character, purpose and value. In other words, 3D Coaches are much more effective in helping their athletes reach their fullest potential both on the field and in life.

"I Want to Do It Right"

In 1985, football coach Jerry Moore lost his job at Texas Tech after going 16-37-2 in five seasons. Not long after that disappointing circumstance, he made this statement:

"If I ever get a head job again, I want to do it right."

Moore was given that chance in 1989 when he was hired as the head coach at Division 1-AA (now the Football Championship Series) Appalachian State. He held true to his intentions and worked towards building the program on 3Dimensional principles. Not only did he implement methods that impacted athletes in the second dimension, but Moore also embarked on a spiritual journey that allowed him to teach his players and coaches about the true meaning behind sports.

By 2005 Appalachian State had won its first national championship. Moore again led the team to a national championship the following year in 2006. Then on September 1, 2007, Appalachian State recorded one of the biggest upsets in college football history when the Mountaineers defeated the fifth-ranked Michigan Wolverines 34-32 at Michigan Stadium. It marked the first time a Football Championship Series (FCS) team had ever defeated a ranked team from the Football Bowl Series (FBS, formerly known as Division 1).

Moore completed a three-peat in that same season by winning the 2007 FCS Championship. Appalachian State also collected 10 Southern Conference titles along the way and Moore finished his career in 2012 with 243 victories. Most important, his players and coaches experienced success in an environment that placed long-term personal relationships as a higher priority over short-term achievement. Moore was able to reap the benefits of 3Dimensional Coaching.

3Dimensional Coaching isn't and should never be about obtaining preferred results. If that's why you're reading this book, then you need to reevaluate what drives you to coach. Instead, the goal of 3Dimensional Coaching should always be to make a difference in the lives of your athletes, your coaches and anyone else who might fall within your circle of influence. The overflow is a higher level of performance from your athletes, which often leads to tangible results.

Watering Seeds

In the biblical parable of the four seeds, Jesus gives us a unique glimpse at what motivation looks like in both the first and second dimensions:

A farmer went out to sow his seed. As he was scattering the seed, some fell along the path, and the birds came and ate it up. Some fell on rocky places, where it did not have much soil. It sprang up quickly, because the soil was shallow. But when the sun came up, the plants were scorched, and they withered because they had no root. Other seed fell among the thorns, which grew up and choked the plants. Still other seed fell on good soil, where it produced a crop—a hundred, sixty or thirty times what was sown (Matt. 13:3-8).

In His time, Jesus spoke to the people where they were in their daily lives. Since many of His audience members were involved in professions such as farming, shepherding and fishing, many of His stories were told in a way that would best relate to them. But if we dive into this particular parable, we can find some interesting analogies for today's sports culture.

The primary message is that we as coaches can't be effective if we don't know our athletes. Here's how that plays out in the case of each of the four seeds and, more important, in the type of ground that each seed falls upon:

1. *The hard ground*: The seed that falls here represents athletes who want to play but who have trouble with commitment. Their motivation was never allowed to take root because they never fully understood why they wanted to play beyond the external rewards that often come with sports.

2. *The rocky ground*: The seed that falls here represents athletes who don't have a support system at home. When difficulty comes their way, they don't have the internal motivation to press through because they lack the true joy that comes from playing sports for the right reasons.

3. *The weeds*: The seed that falls here represents athletes who are constantly faced with problems that keep them from thriving. External pressures, such as family struggles, drug and alcohol use, and sexual temptation, are the thorns that choke out their motivation.

4. *The good soil*: The seed that falls here represents athletes who have a solid foundation and are able to become something great as athletes and as people.

So how can you as a coach plant your athletes in good soil? It takes effort and time, and even then you may not be 100 percent successful. But the key is to get into your athletes' lives and not only become the solid foundation they may not have at home, but also take the time to water the seed. That means getting outside of the first dimension and looking for ways to connect with your athletes on a personal, meaningful level.

The Broader Impact of 3Dimensional Coaching

Before we move one, let's make sure to clear up a myth about holistic coaching and who it does or doesn't impact.

It might be easy to assume that the only athletes who experience second-dimension issues are from low socio-economic environments. While that can be the case, don't be fooled. Kids who have a lot of stuff and come from seemingly good families will also benefit greatly from 3Dimensional Coaching. No one is exempt from deep-seated emotional and spiritual needs. In many cases, the stuff can be hiding the brokenness that they too experience.

IIIIIIIIIIIIIIIIIIIIIIIIIIIIIIIIIIIIIIIIIIIIIIIIIIIIIIIIIIIIIIIIIIIIIIIIIIIIIIIIIIIIIIIIIIIIIIIIIIIIIIII

That's what great leadership is all about—capturing
the hearts of those you lead.

IIIIIIIIIIIIIIIIIIIIIIIIIIIIIIIIIIIIIIIIIIIIIIIIIIIIIIIIIIIIIIIIIIIIIIIIIIIIIIIIIIIIIIIIIIIIIIIIIIIIIIII

This becomes evident as a broken culture is revealed through the tension, pressure, success and failure that sports bring into our lives. We quickly learn about human nature through sports based on the way our athletes, coaches, parents, fans and even we react during the best of times and (even more so) during the worst of times.

On the flipside, think about how easy it would be to coach if all of your players had a great attitude and gave great effort. Then coaching becomes pure joy.

Coaches have an on-field strategy, a practice strategy, an off-season strategy and (for college coaches) a recruiting strategy. But how many coaches have a strategy for capturing the hearts of their athletes? If you don't have a strategy but want to develop one, now is the time to take that first step.

Jesus: The Master Coach

When Jesus of Nazareth launched his ministry in Judea around AD 27, He immediately drew attention to Himself by virtue of the miracles He performed and the unique gospel that He taught. Jesus did most of His teaching in three places: (1) at the water's edge, (2) on a hillside or mountainside, and (3) inside the church, which at that time was the Temple.

The Jewish leaders of the day were like today's first-dimension coaches. From their perspective, salvation was based on performance. But Jesus talked about the heart. These Pharisees and Sadducees, as they were known, had been so mired in the first dimension that they didn't recognize that Jesus was presenting them with a better way—even though it was staring right back into the eyes of their souls. In fact, the religious community became increasingly indignant towards Jesus and eventually conspired with their Roman overlords to have the Son of God put to death.

Here comes this Jesus fellow. I like to call Him the "Master Coach." The first thing He does is put together a team—12 men, to be exact. That sounds a lot like the average-sized basketball squad. And see if this sounds familiar: Jesus had three team captains (Peter, James and John). He had one loud mouth who always spoke out of turn (Peter).

He had some incredible talent (Matthew was good with money; four of His team members turned out to be pretty good writers). Jesus even had a key player who transferred to the rival school right before the championship game just because the other team had more stuff.

Jesus' ministry on Earth was very short. Most Bible scholars believe that it lasted just three-and-a-half years. But those three-and-a-half years were packed with powerful teachings that would impact the world for the next 2,000 years and beyond. Think about it. Jesus spent about the same amount of time that you have with an average four-year class. He showed us coaches that we can model and mentor kids even over a relatively short period of time.

Most important, Jesus displayed a different kind of leadership. He showed what perfect servant leadership and discipleship look like. Jesus unselfishly gave His close circle of followers all the tools they would need to carry on after He was gone. Jesus took time to mentor them and to instill life-giving principles they would share with the masses.

Throughout this book, we will take a look at Jesus' teachings and how we can apply them as 3D Coaches. Through His example, we will better understand that we can no longer reside in the first dimension if we truly want to capture the hearts of our athletes.

Freedom from the First Dimension

As we get deeper into this concept of 3Dimensional Coaching, it is important to first embrace the freedom that comes from moving beyond the first dimension and into the second dimension, and later into what we will identify as the third dimension. Here are three steps that will lead to that freedom:

1. *Realize the impact you have as a coach.* Coaches are the most influential people in the lives of young people today. According to the National Association of Sport and Physical Education, about 43-53 million kids in the United States play or have played organized sports.

At an FCA national coaches' conference in Black Mountain, North Carolina, the world-famous evangelist Billy Graham was conversing with a young man who was struggling with whether or not to stay in coaching.

"I really love coaching, but I know I've got a purpose," he told Dr. Graham. "I'm thinking about going into Christian ministry and church work."

In response, Dr. Graham made this powerful statement: "One coach will impact more young people in one year than the average person will in a lifetime."

Your influence can and should go well beyond the athletic skills you impart to your players. You have the opportunity to make a lasting positive impact on the young people who call you coach.

2. *Be willing to try something different.* We coaches are always looking for the next big thing. In football, many offensive coordinators, for instance, have been swept up in the spread offense craze while defensive coordinators have been forced to tinker with various schemes to slow down their opponents. It's important to have that same kind of innovative, forward-thinking mindset when it comes to the way we approach coaching athletes.

3. *Open your heart to Jesus' example.* Jesus set the ultimate example of 3Dimensional Coaching by depositing spiritual truths into

His team and by tending to their relational needs. He dealt with all of the issues you face as a coach today. There is much to learn from the way He handled the emotional and spiritual needs of His team. Yes, He taught the masses on the mountainsides, on the seashores and in the temples, but He spent most of His time coaching His team—those 12 men. He understood that if He did His job well, they would then spread the message of love and hope all over the world. Talk about a spread offense!

As a coach, you may not have the same calling as those disciples, but what you do isn't really that much different. You have the incredible opportunity to impact young people in a way that very well could change the trajectory of their lives. It's a humbling but equally rewarding calling, should you choose to accept it. And it only gets better as you begin to take the 3Dimensional Coaching principles we are about to study and apply them to your coaching theology.

TRAINING TIME

1. Of the four key second dimension issues (motivation, confidence, emotions and team cohesion), which one seems to give you the most trouble? Give an example of how that issue has impacted you as a coach.
2. Go back and read over the six benefits that accompany 3Dimensional Coaching. Which of these are you most excited to see manifested in your team? Why?
3. In what you presently know about Coach Jesus, what great coaching attributes did He teach?

4. Which of the three steps to freedom to coach beyond the first dimension do you think is easiest to embrace? Which one do you think is the most difficult to live out? Explain.
5. Take some time to write down a few things you hope to get out of the remainder of this book. What areas of your coaching will positively change by becoming a 3D Coach?

PRAYER

Lord, give me the courage to break free from coaching only in the first dimension. Help me fully embrace second dimension principles and begin to coach my athletes the way You coached Your disciples.

7

GETTING THE STUFF

If we were to survey coaches today and ask them about their greatest difficulties in dealing with athletes, there is no doubt that keeping their players motivated would be listed among the most challenging issues. Outside distractions, personal problems and fleeting incentives detract from the average young person's ability to remain motivated over extended periods of time.

Motivation is a second-dimension problem, but most coaches tend to handle second-dimension problems with first-dimension solutions. I, for one, bought into the lie that emotional and mental issues could be worked out with physical solutions. If a kid was late, I made him run laps or push a tire across the field, or I made him give me 20 pushups, just to get his attention. But all I was doing was creating a temporary and unsustainable source of motivation.

As Josh McDowell once said, "Rules without relationship lead to rebellion."

||||||||||||||||||||||||||||||||||||||||||||||||||||||||||||||||||||||||||||||||||||||||||||||||||

We can use physical discipline all day long, but if we
don't move beyond the physical and address the heart
issues that are causing these motivation problems,
we will continue to lose the battle.

||||||||||||||||||||||||||||||||||||||||||||||||||||||||||||||||||||||||||||||||||||||||||||||||||

Dangling Carrots

Today's young athlete is much different than the athlete from 20 or 30 years ago. There are still athletes at all levels who play sports for the sheer enjoyment it brings, but an increasing majority of them play sports because they want to get something out of them. And to make matters worse, many parents have bought into the concept that sports are about the stuff that comes with them.

We see this at all levels. Take for example an average, run-of-the-mill mid-contract NFL holdout story. Entering the 2009 season, Atlanta Falcons receiver Roddy White was set to begin his final year of a five-year contract worth $2.28 million per season. However, after a breakout Pro Bowl effort in 2008, White felt like $2.28 million simply wasn't enough to procure his services. So he declined to report to training camp until the Falcons agreed to draw up a new six-year contract worth $50 million (or roughly $8.3 million per season).

This isn't meant to point a finger at Roddy White. His story is just one of hundreds that dot the professional sports landscape. This is where we are as a culture. Athletes are no longer motivated by the mere joy that comes from playing sports. Rather, they are driven by the promise of external rewards.

And it's not just at a professional level. Let's take it down to the high school level where the promise of collegiate scholarship is increasingly becoming the predominant motivating factor. In a recent NCAA study (2011), it was reported that only 3.4 percent of high school athletes who played varsity sports had received scholarships to play in college. Looking at that in reverse, we see that 96 percent of varsity athletes will *not* be receiving athletic funding to play at the next level.

Yet we, as coaches, are often guilty of dangling college scholarships like a carrot before athletes and their parents. We tell them,

"Work hard, do as I say, and you might have a chance of getting a scholarship by the time you're a senior."

There is absolutely nothing wrong with scholarships. Receiving a scholarship creates a wonderful opportunity for young people who are skilled enough to play beyond high school. However, scholarships should never be used as a means by which coaches motivate their athletes. Instead, they should be the overflow of something those athletes have been motivated to do intrinsically. Their motivation must come from within their hearts. Let's take it down to an even lower level—youth recreational sports. When my sons Matt and Mark were playing little league baseball, I volunteered to help with the signups. As I was sitting at a table, a father showed up with his nine-year-old son.

"How much?" the dad asked me. After I gave him the registration cost, his little boy tapped me on the shoulder and said, "How big is the trophy?"

He hadn't even been placed on a team yet and this nine-year-old boy wanted to know how big the trophy was. Although it was comical at the time, the sad truth is that things like trophies have become the most important part of athletics for young people today.

The Award Ceremony

It seems like everyone gets a trophy. And that's what happens when you coach in the first dimension. Performance-based awards become the quick fix for the larger issues of internal motivation. As the entitlement culture continues to invade the sports culture, it becomes evident that there is never enough money, scholarships, trophies, championships or awards to replace what athletes really need. There has to be a better way!

A few years ago, a colleague and I decided to conduct a study concerning this growing culture of trophies and sports banquets. We learned that two generations ago, if you went to an athletic banquet, there were typically four awards: team MVP, Best Offensive Player, Best Defensive Player and Most Improved. Attend a ceremony today and there will be trophies lined up from one wall to the next. There are all of the aforementioned awards plus Best Sophomore, Best Freshman, the Hustle Award, the Participation Award, Ugliest Kid, Best-Looking Kid. . . the list goes on and on. Whenever it's all about the extrinsic motivators, there will never be enough. You have to keep adding more and more stuff.

Not long ago, a coaching buddy of mine told me what he had done to change the obligatory awards ceremony from something that generates extrinsic motivation to a program that promotes intrinsic motivation. It started out with a simple exercise he gave his seniors at the end of the season. He told them to answer the following two questions on a piece of paper:

1. "What has this program meant to you?"
2. "What did you learn that's going to help you in life?"

The first year, the coaches didn't bother to read the letters beforehand. They just put them into envelopes and had the seniors hand the letters to their parents during the program. Everything else was the same as usual. There were lots of trophies to hand out and a highlight video. But as the event was still going on, the coaches noticed that the parents were distracted. They were reading the letters and in some cases handing them back and forth. They could tell something different was going on.

The second year, they "got fancier" as this coach said. They put the letters on school stationary and mounted them in cheap frames from Walmart. Instead of simply handing the letters to their parents, each senior formally presented it to them in front of the entire audience. The parents loved it. They began reading things about discipline and commitment and serving others.

By the third year, attendance had grown dramatically. The banquet had to move from a restaurant to a larger facility because it wasn't just the parents showing up. It was the grandparents, siblings, aunts and uncles finding themselves drawn to this innovative presentation. The coaches began coordinating the letter-writing efforts with the English department to make sure the senior athletes were doing the best job possible. They mounted the letters in nicer frames. The head coach didn't speak that year. Instead, they showed the year-end highlight video, and then left the lights low for the letter-reading ceremony. As each senior walked to the stage, his parents or guardians would meet him there. With a spotlight on the athlete, he read the letter to them so that the entire audience could hear. The coach recently told me that their awards banquet has become "a crying fest" of tears of joy. As the fourth awards ceremony approached, the head coach decided no longer to give individual trophies or awards in public, but rather to do that privately in the locker room with just the team present. Now, the main focus is on having a great meal together, enjoying a short highlight video and then basking in the emotional glow of these teenage boys sharing their heart with the people closest to them.

You might be thinking, *That's nice and good, but how has it benefited the program?*

According to this coach, something as elementary as a letter-writing exercise has validated the parents and their support of the coaching staff. All of the other parents—those whose kids are juniors, sophomores or freshmen—are thinking, *I can't wait until my kid is a senior*. It becomes much harder for the complaining dad to moan and groan to the coach about his son's playing time when he hears about all the wonderful things this football program has done for so many young athletes. It has eliminated many of the inherent problems that so often occur within a high school sports team.

Quite simply, this coach has created a way that he and his staff can step into the lives of their athletes. He has created a second-dimension strategy for a second-dimension issue.

What's Your Motivation?

Scott Kretchmar once defined motivation as "the inclination to pursue and persist in the journey towards a desired outcome."

In other words, I want it, so I'm going to go after it. As we've already discussed, the motivation exhibited by past generations is quickly fading away. No longer are young athletes satisfied with the concept of playing for fun, self-improvement or the rewarding nature of team achievement. Instead, motivation is based on external and, quite frankly, temporal outcomes.

Before we get into the difference between what we call extrinsic versus intrinsic motivation, let's clarify what it looks like when you do or do not have a motivation problem within your team. It's really quite simple.

High Motivation
- Athlete arrives on time for training.
- Athlete's equipment is in good shape.
- Athlete has good time-management skills.
- Athlete is always ready to try new athletic skills.
- Athlete is willing to memorize.

Low Motivation

- Athlete is regularly late for practice.
- Athlete's equipment is in poor shape.
- Athlete demonstrates poor time-management skills.
- Athlete is unwilling or hesitant to try new skills.
- Athlete doesn't put forth the effort to memorize.

Positive rewards like scholarships, playing time, trophies and awards are among the common strategies that coaches sometimes use to motivate athletes. This is what we refer to as *extrinsic motivation*. And it can sometimes manifest in negative forms such as threat of punishment or coercion. Extrinsic motivation can be identified by any one of these three dynamics:

1. *It is imposed by external factors.* When athletes perform well, they believe they should get something in return.
2. *It results in introjection.* Athletes begin to internalize the belief that external rewards are the primary goal.
3. *It plays into one's identification.* Eventually, athletes begin to base their identity on performance.

The opposite is called *intrinsic motivation*, which we will discuss at greater length in the next chapter. Just like it sounds, intrinsic motivation is produced from within the individual and is driven by an interest in or enjoyment of the sport itself. As mentioned earlier, however, our sports society has become more defined by external forces.

So here is an important question that we all should ask ourselves as it pertains to the way we motivate our athletes: Are we dangling carrots or are we watering seeds?

If you want to dangle carrots (scholarships and awards), prepare to deal with the reality that those promises, even when realized, are ultimately empty and do little to satisfy one's soul. If you want to rely solely on first-dimension methods of discipline and fear, prepare to experience what Josh McDowell said about "rules without relationship."

But if you want to move into a higher level of coaching, remember what we talked about in chapter 6: Take time to guide the seeds (your athletes) towards the good soil (a solid foundation) and then take time to water those seeds until they begin to grow and bear fruit.

When the Stuff Runs Out

A couple of thousand years before the first professional sporting event ever took place, Jesus was teaching His team about the difference between extrinsic and intrinsic motivation. People in those days were just as enamored with getting the stuff as we are today. To illustrate the point, Jesus told a story about a man and his two sons. The complete story can be found in Luke 15:11-32, but here's a brief summary:

> The father was wealthy and the younger son wanted his inheritance before he had reached the required age. The son was impatient. He wanted to explore the world. He demanded the inheritance and his father gave it to him.
>
> The son took off and did what a lot of young people do if you give them money before they're mature enough to handle it. He blew it.
>
> He partied and did all kinds of things, but then one day, he woke up and realized he was broke. He had nowhere to stay and no food to eat. It got so bad for this young man that he ended up in a pigsty.

"I have to go home," he said to himself. "My father's servants live better than this. Maybe he'll let me come back and be one of his servants."

So the humbled son made his way back home. As he walked that final stretch of road, his father, who had never stopped worrying, saw him from a distance. The father ran as fast as he could to meet his son and lovingly embraced him. He instantly forgave his son and welcomed him back into the family.

What an incredible story of grace. I don't know where you are in your coaching journey or how far you've gotten away from the essence of what you're supposed to be doing. This parable is an illustration of how much God loves us and how He wants us to come home. And when we do, He will take us back with open arms.

But that's only half of the story.

The other half contains an interesting correlation to the coaching world. There was an older brother in the story and he never left home. He was a great first-dimensional son. He performed all the duties required of him at the house. He did everything he was supposed to do. When his brother returned, he wasn't as excited as his father. In fact, he was upset because his father threw a huge party for the younger son. The father dressed the younger son in select pieces from his own upscale wardrobe and fancy shoe collection. The young man even got to drive the black Escalade. Your Bible version of the story might say something about a fatted calf, a robe and a ring, but let's just put it this way: The older brother felt like he was getting the shaft. And he couldn't stand it!

When the father realized his oldest son wasn't at the party, he found him and asked him to join the other guests.

"Your younger brother is home!" he said. "I thought he was dead! But he's alive and well!"

"I can't," the older brother muttered. "I just can't."

He couldn't come to the party because his life was based on stuff. It was not based on relationship with his dad and with his brother. The older brother was so jealous and so full of moral outrage that he chose not to participate in what should have been a celebratory event.

That is what has happened in our sports culture. It's become all about the stuff. That has become the motivation for many athletes and coaches today. Don't get me wrong; there's nothing wrong with scholarships or professional contracts. Such things are great when they can be obtained. But they should be the overflow because the vast majority of athletes are not going to get to that level.

|||||||||||||||||||||||||||||||||||||||||||||||||||||||||||||||||||||||||||||||||||||||||||||||||||||||||

It doesn't matter if we're talking about sports or life in general. There is never enough stuff to take the place of meaningful relationships. And when the stuff runs out, that's when it becomes painfully obvious that there has to be more.

|||||||||||||||||||||||||||||||||||||||||||||||||||||||||||||||||||||||||||||||||||||||||||||||||||||||||

As coaches, we must resist the temptation to build our programs on the shaky foundation of extrinsic motivation and learn to lead from the heart.

TRAINING TIME

1. In this chapter, we listed five ways a coach can recognize that he or she has a motivational issue with an athlete (see "What's Your Motivation?"). Have you seen any of these issues with your athletes? If so, how have you typically tried to correct the problem?
2. What are some healthy benefits to using extrinsic motivation when working with athletes?
3. What are some of the limitations or negative outcomes associated with extrinsic motivation?
4. How have you been able to utilize intrinsic motivation thus far in your coaching career? What benefits came from that approach?

PRAYER

Lord, help me resist the temptation of using awards and temporal things to motivate my athletes. Teach me to build the kinds of relationships that will last long after they have moved beyond my influence as their coach.

8

OPEN HEART POLICY

If you've been around and coaching for very long, you've probably heard a variation of this line a time or two:

> Hey, guys! I just want you to know that I have an open door policy. If you ever need to talk about anything, don't hesitate to stop by my office anytime. I'm here for you.

I'm sure many coaches who say this are sincere when they give the speech. Others perhaps announce the open door policy because it's what they think they're supposed to do.

How do I know this? I used to give that speech every year.

In reality, most athletes rarely take their coaches up on the offer. That's because the coaches haven't stepped into their players' lives in a meaningful way. They haven't taken time to mentor them. They haven't shown them that they truly care about them apart from what they can do on the field of play.

I'm not quite sure how I fell into this trap as a young coach. I had great parental influence, a solid high school mentor (Coach Corbett), and a legendary 3D Coach (Coach Bowden) as role models in my early career. Still, I struggled to find peace and contentment as a coach. I failed to understand, much less grasp, this concept of capturing the heart behind the jersey.

That speaks volumes to the gravitational pull of a broken sports culture. I had allowed pride to gradually creep in until it had finally consumed my ego. Outside of my stint with FCA, every next step offered me a little bit more—more money, more prestige, more power. Before long, I compromised my identity in Christ and conformed to "the pattern of this world" as the apostle Paul wrote about in Romans 12:2. All the while, the world seemingly applauded every career move I made.

This mindset stunted my ability to coach in the second and third dimensions. I was stuck in the first dimension because that's where I was in control. That's where performance was king. That's where I had misplaced my identity. And it drove me crazy.

As a young coach, my strategy was very simple. If I wanted a team to play great together, I bought everyone a T-shirt. Each year, I'd put motivational quotes or phrases on them to encourage unity:

There is no I in TEAM
BIG TEAM, little me
One Heartbeat

That was my strategy. I gave the kids a shirt and they wore it. My hope was that the words on the fabric would fuse into who they were as people by some strange form of osmosis. It was pretty weak, but it was all I had.

|||||||||||||||||||||||||||||||||||||||||||||||||||||||||||||||||||||||||||||||||||||||||||||||||||||

You can escape the broken sports culture and forge a better, healthier, more joyful path.

|||||||||||||||||||||||||||||||||||||||||||||||||||||||||||||||||||||||||||||||||||||||||||||||||||||

I imagine most of you reading this can relate to what I'm talking about. It's a trap that can ensnare any of us if we're not careful. And if you feel as if it's too late, as though you've already fallen into the pit and can't get back out, be encouraged by my story.

Getting in the Boat

As we embark on this journey into the second dimension, we can look to Jesus' example for an incredible tool that will help us motivate our athletes—serving others. Yes, coaches have the responsibility of directing young people on the practice field and during game situations, but Jesus tells us we are to serve those who are under our leadership. This is how He conveyed that message to His disciples:

> You know that the rulers of the Gentiles lord it over them, and their high officials exercise authority over them. Not so with you. Instead, whoever wants to become great among you must be your servant, and whoever wants to be first must be your slave—just as the Son of Man did not come to be served, but to serve, and to give his life as a ransom for many (Matt. 20:25-28).

Jesus modeled servant leadership by pouring into the lives of His disciples. He most certainly healed the sick and preached to the masses, but the majority of His time was spent with those 12 men. He had a strategy for entering into His team members' lives.

In fact, it started at the very beginning. When Jesus first started His ministry, He went to the seaside on a recruiting trip. His first four prospects were fisherman: Peter, Andrew, James and John. Jesus went down to the water where they were working. He even got into the boat with Peter and helped him fish. Jesus spoke their language. He talked about what was important to them and He used fishing as a way to share His game plan.

The same is true for coaches who want to reside in the second dimension. It is the place where we can begin to show our players that we care.

||||||||||||||||||||||||||||||||||||||||||||||||||||||||||||||||||||||||||||||||||||||||||||||||||||||||||||||||||

We get in the boat. We get involved in their lives, and that's when things start to change.

||||||||||||||||||||||||||||||||||||||||||||||||||||||||||||||||||||||||||||||||||||||||||||||||||||||||||||||||||

Motivation is no longer driven by external forces but by internal things. Motivation now takes place from the inside out. We call this *intrinsic motivation*. Here's what it looks like for the athlete:

- Sport is now fun. It feels good.
- Sport now creates an intrinsic (or internal) motivation toward accomplishments. Motivation is no longer driven by external rewards.
- Sport now creates a clear desire to experience emotional stimulation.
- Sport now creates an internal motivation to know more about big picture things, such as the meaning of life.

As we talked about in a previous chapter, this all starts when we take time to show athletes that we care about them away from the game. When we utilize extrinsic motivation to get the desired performance from our athletes, the outcomes might be positive in the short-term, but over time those external things we offer up as rewards will no longer be enough. There has to be something deeper that drives them to pursue excellence on the field and in their personal lives.

The First-Dimension Parent Trap

One of the biggest lessons I learned about stepping into the lives of athletes didn't actually take place on the football field. It happened in my home.

My wife and I are very different. Dana is very musical and artistic. In fact, she now teaches music and art at an elementary school. Dana truly sees the flow of life. On the other hand, I'm very linear. I see life in first downs, goal lines and touchdowns. Our personality differences were especially evident early on when we were young parents.

With my oldest son, Bo, I tended to parent as if I was a first-dimension coach. I loved him dearly but I demonstrated that love in ways that didn't always connect with his personality. Bo was more like Dana. He was very musical and non-linear in his approach to life, yet I was always parenting him in the first dimension. It was a real struggle to get him to respond.

Bo went off to college ready to take on the world. But in three attempts, he only completed three credit hours. (In the college world, that's not very good.) So he decided to move to Nashville and then on to Los Angeles to pursue a career in music. It was an interesting time. I knew he was hanging out in places that weren't healthy for him. To make it in the music business, you have to play late into the night in clubs and bars and hole-in-the-wall dives. Whenever we touched base, I could tell it was wearing on him.

I didn't really know what to say to motivate him. So I went back to some of the research I had done. What I had discovered is that the younger generations today need an authority figure to step into their lives and let them know that they genuinely care about them. It's not about trying to change them or doing something for them. They need to see your presence.

I reflected on the story of how Jesus formed His team. He didn't yell out to Peter and Andrew from the shoreline, "Hey, guys! You fishermen out there! Come over here with me! I have a plan!"

Instead, Jesus got into the boat with them. He helped them catch some fish on a day when fish were nowhere to be found. He mesmerized them. He stepped into their lives and captured their hearts. And then, when He asked them to join Him on this journey—this mission to fish for men—they immediately got on board with the plan. They willingly left their environment to follow His lead.

After reading these things, I became very convicted. I jumped on an airplane and flew out to Los Angeles where Bo resided in yet another effort to get his career going. I hadn't spoken to him in a while other than a few brief phone conversations. When we met for dinner, I felt the need to air things out.

"Son, I just need to apologize," I told him.

"What for?" he replied with a confused look.

"All these years, I've been trying to make you into something that I thought you ought to be," I explained. "What I've realized is that you are already something special and I need to allow you to become the person *God* wants you to be."

Bo jumped in before I could continue. "Oh no, Dad! You and Mom have loved me and given me a great home!"

"I know," I quickly responded. "I know we gave you the stuff. But I didn't allow you to be who you are. I just wanted to come out here and tell you that."

A few months later, Bo came home for Christmas. While he was in town, we went to church for the Christmas Eve service. That night, the worship leader was playing with a four-piece band. The music had a more modern feel and the band was doing a great job. I noticed Bo seemed to really enjoy what he was experiencing. Afterwards, he even commented on how good the music was.

I introduced my son to the worship leader and they hit it off. Towards the end of the conversation, the worship leader asked Bo if he'd like to sit in with the band for the next couple of weeks while he was in town. And he did. Not long after that, I talked to the worship leader about how things were going.

"Jeff, he's really good," he said.

"I know," I responded, "I just wish he could find his way."

"You know there are schools out there just for guys like Bo," he said.

I had no idea there were schools that focused solely on music ministry, so I went to Bo to talk about it. Apparently, he already knew about these institutions. The next thing I knew, he was talking to my wife and me about some options, including one that seemed far-fetched at first glance. Bo was interested in attending the Hillsong International Leadership College in Australia, which was founded by the world-renowned Hillsong Church.

For a brief moment, I slipped back into first-dimension mode.

"Australia! How much is that going to cost?" I blurted.

But then I looked into it, and it wasn't that bad. It was only about $5,000 a year to attend. The bigger expense was the travel and housing. More important, my son had made a life-changing discovery. Bo spent the next two years in Australia living on his own. He returned with a degree and began serving at a church as a worship leader in central Florida.

For several months, my wife and I attended that church. I would stand in the auditorium as my son played music and led the congregation in worship. With tears rolling down my face, I couldn't help but think about what had ultimately made the difference in his life:

I told him how much I cared. That's all it took. Because of that simple gesture, Bo stepped back into our world and found his place. I was his father. I was the authority figure in his life.

Coaches, you have that same weight with your athletes.

||||||||||||||||||||||||||||||||||||||||||||||||||||||||||||||||||||||||||||||||||||||||||||||||||||

It wasn't about doing something great.
It was about being present.

||||||||||||||||||||||||||||||||||||||||||||||||||||||||||||||||||||||||||||||||||||||||||||||||||||

The Power of Presence

My second son, Cameron, is more like me. He's a coach. He has the same passion that I had as a young coach, but he also watched me go through my struggles. He thankfully learned about being a 3D Coach much earlier in his career than I did.

In 2010, a big program in north Florida was making some changes. The new superintendent had learned about 3Dimensional Coaching and wanted to hire a head coach who would lead by those values. The new coach hired Cameron as his offensive coordinator. The previous year, the team struggled to a 1-9 record. The kids weren't motivated. They lacked great attitude and effort. It was going to be a significant challenge to turn things around.

On the first day, the head coach told his assistants something unusual.

"Guys, don't forget. We all need to be sure to visit the house of every athlete we coach. I want you to spend at least 15 minutes with each family."

Cameron was assigned two brothers who lived in a very low socio-economic area. Alphonso and Lenorris were their names. Alphonso was a running back. His younger brother, Lenorris, was a quarterback. Lenorris was a good athlete but had missed 23 days of school the previous year. He was very unmotivated and only showed up when he wanted to show up. When my son told the brothers that he wanted to meet their family, the young men weren't terribly crazy about the idea.

"Coach, you don't need to do that!" they insisted.

"No, guys," Cameron replied. "That's my job as your coach. I'm coming by tomorrow to meet your family."

Picture this: After getting permission from the principal, my blonde-haired, blue-eyed son, a product of suburbia, drove those two African-American boys to their rural home. It was like oil and water. The entire way home Lenorris and Alphonso reminded Cameron that he didn't need to come inside the house to visit their family. When Cameron first shared this story with me, he admitted he was a little nervous. He had never done this before. His experience visiting this family was his first.

What was supposed to be a 15-minute meeting turned into a two-hour affair. Cameron made an incredible connection with the boys' mother, their aunts and some of their cousins. The mom was clearly thankful that one of the coaches had taken the time to sit in her living room and talk about her boys. What mother doesn't enjoy hearing someone else tell her how talented her kids are and how much potential they have? After that meeting, Lenorris never missed school again. He eventually accepted a scholarship to play at Alcorn State.

As the new coaching staff began to turn that team around, they did all of the first-dimension things that are required to produce quality football. But it wasn't a secret offense or a secret weight program that made the difference. It was a connection. It was being present.

Two years into the new coaching staff's tenure, the team won a state championship. This group of unmotivated kids was now motivated to reach their fullest potential and they jelled as a team. I wish I could say that this is always the case—that motivating athletes in the second dimension will always produce championships. That's obviously not possible. But athletes *will* play at a higher level.

The parents will change too. My son saw this firsthand as parental support increased. The coaches didn't fix any problems. They didn't repair any relationships. They didn't create jobs for anyone either. They were simply present. And they genuinely cared.

When Lennoris was a senior, the team had a great season. I was able to attend their third-round playoff game. After a tough loss, I walked behind the stadium where my son's team buses were parked. I'll never forget what I saw. Cameron and Lennoris were embracing each other like long lost friends. Both were in tears. Then I realized what was happening. It was the end of the season and the end of Lennoris's high school career. This was the athlete and his coach's last time together. Cameron had stepped into that young man's life and made a lasting impact in the process.

It might seem radical at first, but doing something as simple as visiting each athlete at home can change the motivation of an entire team. If you decide to try this with your program, make sure to first get permission from the athletic director or the principal before you proceed. If you coach a large team, like my son's football squad, split the team up among your assistant coaches. You don't have to be a psychologist. You don't have to fix all of your athletes' problems. You just have to show them you care. A first-dimension coach might see it as a waste of time, but a second-dimension coach will say it's the most valuable thing he can do.

Cameron's story is a perfect example of what it looks like to turn an open door policy into an "open heart" policy. It's not about having a depth of knowledge. It's as simple as genuinely stepping into your athletes' lives.

||||||||||||||||||||||||||||||||||||||||||||||||||||||||||||||||||||||||||||||||||||||||||||||||||||

Jesus had a plan. For the Master Coach, that meant getting in the boat. For you, it might mean visiting your athletes at their homes.

||||||||||||||||||||||||||||||||||||||||||||||||||||||||||||||||||||||||||||||||||||||||||||||||||||

But there's much more to it than that. It's important to go even deeper and discover what it looks like to foster intrinsic motivation within the greater context of your sport—both on the practice field and on the field of play.

TRAINING TIME

1. Reread Matthew 20:25-28. How does Coach Jesus' approach to leadership differ from the world's approach?
2. How does that Scripture personally challenge you as a coach?
3. How do you think meeting with each of your athletes where they live might change the overall motivation of your team?
4. What are some other ideas you have that will help you enter into the lives of your athletes?

PRAYER

Lord, I want to enter into the lives of my athletes. I want to show them that I truly care about them as individuals. Give me the wisdom that will allow me to make a significant impact. Help me build healthy relationships with them that will motivate them to reach their fullest potential and pursue a relationship with You.

9

SUPER MODELING

Amazing things happen when you enter into the lives of your athletes and start to see extrinsic motivation shift towards the more meaningful intrinsic motivation. In the last chapter we focused on ways to develop those relationships off the field, but now let's get into some practical application.

One of the most effective ways to encourage intrinsic motivation is through *modeling*. Research shows that this is the best way to create leadership in today's culture. There are three basic types of modeling and they all work together in order to help athletes rely less on external motivations and become more driven by internal stimulus.

Leader Modeling is the first and most basic form of modeling. As coaches, we all do this as a regular part of our training regimen. We set the practices. We set the drills. We maintain our authority over the team. This form of modeling allows us to do what we're called to do: teach our athletes specific tasks and train them to perform. But the problem is when we stay in the first dimension and never step outside of leader modeling.

There is so much that can be achieved when we allow our athletes to take part in *Peer Modeling*. This form of modeling happens after you establish your authority as the coach. You might say it's the positive side of peer pressure.

||||||||||||||||||||||||||||||||||||||||||||||||||||||||||||||||||||||||||||||||||||||||||||||||

Peer modeling takes place when you take athletes who
are good at a particular skill and have them help teach
the ones who aren't as good.

||||||||||||||||||||||||||||||||||||||||||||||||||||||||||||||||||||||||||||||||||||||||||||||||

What happens then is that you will start to see a higher level of cognitive skill learning. There's just something different that takes place when young people learn from other young people. It becomes easier for them to visualize themselves competently performing that skill. This isn't just true in athletics. It's true in everyday life. In fact, it was something I had unwittingly learned years earlier with my oldest son, Bo.

When he was six years old, my wife and I left Bo with another family while we went out of town for three days. Bo was in what I like to call a whiny stage of his adolescence and he quite frankly didn't have very good manners. Being from the south, we tried our hardest to teach all of our boys to say, "Yes, sir," "Yes, Ma'am" and "Thank you," but for some reason Bo wasn't catching on as fast as we would have preferred. At times, I was tempted to use discipline to force him to have better manners, but nothing seemed to work.

When we picked him up, Bo turned to his hostess and said, "Ma'am, thank you for letting me stay with you."

My wife and I looked at each other, stunned, as if to say, "Is this our kid?"

The next morning back at our home, Dana put together what we call the "elementary school breakfast," which is a quick bowl of cereal and some toast if you're lucky. It was our way of making up for lost time and getting the kids out the door and off to school. After Bo took his last bite, he politely thanked his mother for making his meal. We were flabbergasted!

So what had changed? How had my son suddenly learned to have manners? Quite simply, Bo was the product of peer modeling. He spent three days around another young boy who had good manners and learned those skills for himself.

The idea of allowing athletes to teach other athletes is frightening to a first-dimension coach. It sounds more like losing control than like anything remotely productive. But if they are teaching each other what *you* have taught them (and if you have taught them well), then it becomes a transformative process within your team.

Here's a small example of how peer modeling has impacted one of our teams. During the 2013 season, my first year as the passing coach at South Lake High School, we had a quarterback named Nick Gadetty. Up to that point, I had coached Nick for five years dating back to his Pop Warner days. In 2012, he was our junior varsity quarterback, but he had now moved up to the starting varsity position.

Nick was one of the quietest kids I've ever coached, but he was a really good kid. After years of modeling relational leadership to Nick, we finally saw him come out of his shell. Now, he comes over to the sidelines and tells *us* what plays the opposing defense is making available.

"Coach! I can throw the backside fade! They're playing inside-out leverage on our receiver!"

It was amazing to hear these things coming out of his mouth. He was just 16 years old yet he felt the confidence to discuss play calling with an authority figure. That's what it looks like when an athlete has experienced solid leader and peer modeling. After a while, it becomes an everyday occurrence.

Here's another powerful story about peer modeling:

In 2010, one of my good friends (and coach of a football team in the Orlando area) sat in on a clinic where I was speaking.

He came to me afterwards and told me he was going to try peer modeling with his players. Traditionally, his team had been pretty good, but that season his players had struggled early to a mediocre 2-2 record. They ran an offense that occasionally utilized a misdirection play with two wings and a dive back. The guard had the key block. On this particular play, they wanted to run the counter in both directions with two slot backs. But to do that, they needed to pull a guard on both sides.

The coach had a senior guard who wasn't much of a leader, but he could trap block really well. On the other side, he had a sophomore guard who was a little bigger, stronger and quicker, but his technique wasn't very good. So the offense could only run the play in one direction. It didn't take long for teams to figure out which way they would run the ball on the counter.

One day, the coach brought the senior guard into his office. This young man had rarely spoken in his time with the program. But the coach decided to ask him if he would take the sophomore guard and work with him. Of course, the kid said yes. Kids will do anything a coach asks them to do.

The next day in practice, the senior worked with the younger player on individual line blocking drills. He was even using a dummy bag to help the sophomore get his steps down just right. After 10 minutes, the team broke into a scrimmage and the counter play was called. This time, however, the sophomore guard hit the outside linebacker perfectly and the slot back got loose for a 35-yard gain.

The following Friday night, the team was facing third and seven at midfield. The coach called the counter play and that sophomore guard once again blocked his defender and allowed the slot back to jaunt 48 yards for a touchdown.

There are 11 players on a football team. Eight players went to celebrate with the slot back in the end zone. That's nine players. So where were the other two? Back at the line of scrimmage, the senior guard was hugging the sophomore guard. He was excited to watch his teammate do something well that he'd taught him. That senior had learned to serve someone else, and the result of serving his teammate was a success.

The following Monday, the elder lineman showed up in the coach's office. He was visibly excited and wanted to know if he could do anything else to help. This quiet young man suddenly became one of the most vocal players on the team. He became self-motivated because he was asked to do what he was already good at and help someone else get better in the process. That young man was taught how to serve and was subsequently released into a new realm of leadership.

From that point on, the coach ran his entire practices with peer modeling. And as a side note, the team went on to win the state championship. I need to be careful, of course, not to dangle winning a championship out there as a carrot for what modeling can do for a team. It will, however, bring out the best in your athletes.

The final step in this process should lead us to what we call *self-modeling*. This takes place when the athlete becomes self-motivated to pursue excellence at a particular skill after he has internalized what he has seen modeled by others.

And ultimately, it's not about the team's success on the field, but rather it's about the atmosphere of service that becomes the overflow of second-dimension modeling. As Craig Groeschel, pastor of one of America's largest churches, once said:

Delegating tasks creates followers. Delegating authority creates leaders.

At the end of the day, that's what this coaching profession is really all about: building up the next generation of leaders. But they will never get the chance to truly lead if we don't provide that opportunity on the practice field and on the playing field. From there, it will naturally spill over into the classroom, into the community and into their homes.

Walking on Water

We can learn even more about modeling as we look deeper into Jesus' time on Earth. For three years, He established Himself as the greatest leader-modeler in history. There is no better example of this than in Matthew 14:22-33. After Jesus famously fed 5,000 followers with just two loaves of bread and five pieces of fish, He told the disciples to get into their boat and meet Him on the other side of the lake.

Just before dawn, Jesus modeled the miraculous once again. He walked on the water towards them.

> They were terrified. "It's a ghost!" they said, and cried out in fear. But Jesus immediately said to them: "Take courage! It is I. Don't be afraid" (Matt. 14:26-27).

While the others cowered, one disciple saw this as an opportunity.

> "Lord, if it's you," Peter replied, "tell me to come to you on the water."
> "Come," he said.

Then Peter got down out of the boat, walked on the water and came toward Jesus (Matt. 14:28-29).

We know the rest of that story. Peter sees the wind and allows fear to distract him, but Jesus reaches out and saves him from drowning. As they climb into the boat, the other disciples are now, more than ever, convinced that Jesus is the Son of God. But it didn't happen until they saw one of their own get out of the boat and walk on the water with Him.

As time passed, there was no longer any doubt in the disciples' minds that Jesus was in charge. "All authority has been given to Me in heaven and on earth," He proclaimed in Matthew 28:18.

But Jesus didn't use that authority to rule over His followers in a heavy-handed manner. Instead, He chose to entrust them and empower them through peer modeling. Just before Jesus ascended into heaven, He released the disciples to duplicate and multiply His ministry:

Go, therefore, and make disciples of all nations, baptizing them in the name of the Father and of the Son and of the Holy Spirit, teaching them to observe everything I have commanded you. And remember, I am with you always, to the end of the age (Matt. 28:19-20).

Over the next several months, His followers did exactly as He commanded. Later, a man named Saul (who had been persecuting the followers of Christ) was converted to the Christian faith in a radical way. He changed his name to Paul and was mentored by other Christians and eventually came to a point where he was able to reach the level of self-modeling.

Paul's self-motivation allowed him to endure many hardships along the way, and he quickly came full circle to the point of becoming in influential leader-modeler for the Early Church. His transformation was evident in writings such as this:

> I discipline my body and bring it under strict control, so that after preaching to others, I myself will not be disqualified (1 Cor. 9:27).

This is the same goal we coaches should have for our athletes—that they become self-motivated to serve their teammates and to one day become successful leader-modelers in their own right.

TRAINING TIME

1. As a coach, is it easy for you to delegate responsibility to others? Why or why not?
2. What are some ways you have been able to utilize peer modeling with your athletes and how did it impact their performance individually and as a team?
3. Why do you think self-modeling is so effective in helping an athlete learn a skill or behavior? How do you think self-modeling can help an athlete later in life?
4. Why do you think Coach Jesus delegated such an important task to His followers?
5. Take some time to brainstorm more ways you can implement peer modeling in your coaching. What do you expect to see happen as a result of this style of second-dimension leadership?

PRAYER

Lord, thank You for demonstrating the power of peer modeling with Your disciples. Help me to loosen the reigns of my authority and allow my athletes to serve each other on and off the field. Give me the creativity I need to implement these concepts with my team so that they will become self-motivated, strong pillars of leadership, and a positive influence wherever their lives may take them.

10

RESTORING CONFIDENCE

Early in my coaching career, I was the JV Head Coach at Zephyrhills High School. During one particular game, our return man fumbled the opening kickoff but recovered the ball near our own goal line. On the first play, I called a fade route. All we had to do to successfully execute the play was to make sure that our guards did their jobs in gap protection.

The ball was snapped and everything went perfectly with one huge exception. Our right guard forgot to block down. That allowed the other team's defensive lineman to sack our quarterback, David Coin, who was left helpless in the end zone. David fumbled and the other team recovered the ball for a touchdown. Just two plays into the game and we were already down 6-0. The team ran over to the sidelines where I was waiting for them. True to form, I did what any good first-dimension coach would do. I yelled at them.

"What is going on out there? Simplest play we could run! What's going on?"

Of the 11 kids on the field, 10 of them did exactly what they were supposed to do. Did the right guard need to be reminded that he needed to do his job next time? Absolutely. That is a first-dimension solution to a first-dimension problem. But even then, it should have been done in an encouraging manner and in a way that rebuilt his confidence and didn't tear it down.

Instead of seeing 10 things that were done well and reminding them of that fact, I unnecessarily focused on what was wrong. I was blinded by the wrong and never saw the right.

At the time, I couldn't see what I was doing, but my blow-up on the sidelines created a fear of failure. With just a few angry words, I destroyed the confidence of that offense for the rest of the game. I should have reinforced the confidence of the 10 players who did their job well and then privately corrected the one who made a mistake.

That doesn't mean telling a player he did great when he messed up. That's lying. Simply put, the coach must specifically affirm what is right and honorably correct what is wrong.

In that moment, however, I didn't take into account the fact that what we as coaches say and do *will* affect our athletes one way or another. Vince Lombardi said it best:

Confidence is contagious. So is lack of confidence.

Confidence is a tricky thing. It's kind of like character. It takes time to build it up, but it can be torn down in an instant.

I've spent a good portion of my career coaching quarterbacks. I like to think that I've become pretty good at identifying mechanical problems that come up occasionally. For instance, if one of my quarterbacks has a sagging elbow and an open hip on a simple hitch route, I know where the ball is headed. It's going off to the right and about four rows up into the stands.

Whether it's in practice, at halftime or during the offseason, I'm going to have to work with that quarterback on foot drills, on getting his hips squared up and on getting his elbow up. Those are all first-dimension problems that need first-dimension solutions.

But sometimes, it's not just a problem with mechanics. There is often an issue with the athlete's confidence. Lack of confidence is a second-dimension problem and it can't be fixed in the first dimension. You have to go deeper in order to restore an athlete's confidence. And if you don't, the second half of Lombardi's assessment is much more likely to come true. A lack of confidence is dangerously contagious and can spread throughout an entire team if not dealt with quickly and at its root.

Skill vs. Belief

Within the context of sports performance, *confidence* is defined as one of the most influential psychological contributors to success on the playing field for an athlete or a team. It is an individual's belief that he or she has the necessary skills to produce a desired outcome.

When confidence is shaken or completely lost, the athlete's mindset is challenged with this nagging thought: *I could do it before, but I can't do it as well now.* There is no doubt that an athlete must continue to work on the fundamentals of physical performance during this time. After all, the concept of skill is rooted in the first dimension. But belief is much deeper than that. And in order to regain confidence—that sense of belief—the athlete must be led down a path within the second dimension.

Nebraska women's volleyball coach John Cook can relate to this common problem. Despite coaching one of the best teams in the country, he was still dealing with a significant lack of confidence among his talented athletes. It was so bad that Cook, an NCAA championship coach and national coach of the year, was beginning to question his coaching prowess despite being at the peak of his career.

"The issue isn't volleyball," Cook explained. "Things break in their lives and they bring it to the court and it affects their performance. I can't fix it and it's driving me nuts!" So Cook decided to take a look at some 3Dimensional Coaching methods on confidence. About a month later, it had already started to work wonders with his team.

||||||||||||||||||||||||||||||||||||||||||||||||||||||||||||||||||||||||||||||||||||||||||||||||||||||

"I don't know who it changed more—me or them,"
he said. "They still have problems, but I've been able
to help them regain confidence in their abilities."

||||||||||||||||||||||||||||||||||||||||||||||||||||||||||||||||||||||||||||||||||||||||||||||||||||||

Coach Cook did some very simple things that helped demonstrate the connection between skill and belief. Let's take a look at the same principles that you too can apply when faced with confidence issues on your team.

Three Steps to Restoring Confidence

Second-dimension coaching is perhaps no more countercultural and counterintuitive than it is when dealing with an athlete's confidence. Our first instinct is to fall back on first-dimension solutions. I have been the chief of sinners on this principle. When coaching baseball, for instance, I might have had a kid who started to struggle with the curve ball. For some reason, he had lost confidence in his ability to do what he could do well before. So what would I have told him when he whiffed badly during batting practice?

"C'mon, Johnny! You can hit better than that!"

I've since learned the powerful nature of what comes out of my mouth. As a coach, my words have great influence. They can have both a positive and a negative impact on my athletes' confidence levels. And it goes beyond words and into actions. Here's what it looks like when a coach tries to fix a second-dimension problem (confidence) with first-dimension solutions:

- The coach reminds the athlete of past failures (uses negative statements such as, "Quit doing that!").
- The coach encourages the athlete to watch others' failures (this plays into the reality show and tabloid culture that seeks to elevate one's self by watching others fail).
- The coach verbally discourages the athlete (uses devaluing statements such as, "You can't do it!").

Right or wrong, these solutions might have been effective two or three generations ago, but they don't work anymore. Our homes are not as strong as they once were. The family unit is no longer a place where young people are continually built up. Certainly, the home is still the best place for motivation and confidence, but when that goes away, it falls to coaches to instill those values into the youth culture. Former San Francisco 49ers head coach Bill Walsh said it this way:

People thrive on positive reinforcement. They can take only a certain amount of criticism and you may lose them altogether if you criticize them in a personal way. You can make a point without being personal. Don't insult or belittle your people. Instead of getting more out of them you will get less.

Let's take a look at three second-dimension solutions that will restore confidence in your athletes:

1. *Performance accomplishments*: Take your athletes back to a time when they did a particular skill well. Show them their past successes through video analysis, verbal storytelling or visualization.
2. *Vicarious experiences*: Watch others successfully perform the skill. Have the athlete watch video or point out their peers who are doing that skill well in practice and in games.
3. *Verbal persuasion*: Encourage the athlete with your words. Be specific in your affirmation. When a player does something wrong—like a bad block—we are quick to say things like, "C'mon, man! Get your arm around! Set your feet! Get your head up!" But when a kid does something well, we say thinks like, "Good job, son! Way to go! Way to hang in there!" Those generalities mean nothing to an athlete. Tell them exactly what they did well.

When you do these things, resist the temptation to use flattery. Flattery is lying to them. Instead, honestly assess where they are and do it in a way that builds them up and doesn't tear them down. And don't stop there.

|||||||||||||||||||||||||||||||||||||||||||||||||||||||||||||||||||||||||||||||||||||||||||||||||||||||

Create an environment within your program
where the other coaches and the players also engage
in verbal encouragement.

|||||||||||||||||||||||||||||||||||||||||||||||||||||||||||||||||||||||||||||||||||||||||||||||||||||||

If you have coaches who are negative, tell them to stop. If they refuse to do so, get rid of them. Likewise, make it very clear to your athletes that negative talk about teammates has no place on the team.

When you start to use these simple techniques (and rid your program of negative elements), you will be amazed what happens to the confidence level of your athletes who struggle with their skill performance. Yes, we still need to help them fix technical issues in the first dimension, but help can't stop there. Be prepared to step into their hearts and help them reclaim the joy that they have lost. You have that kind of influence. You can be the catalyst for renewed confidence in your athletes.

Confidence for Life

The real beauty of building confidence in the second dimension is found in the long-term nature of its principles. When we help athletes regain confidence, we not only help them improve their performance but we also give them a blueprint for how they can have confidence in the future and how they can instill confidence in others when they take on leadership roles of their own.

It should be no surprise that these concepts are thousands of years old and based in biblical truths dating back to Moses and continuing through the life of Jesus and His followers.

For instance, when the Israelites were faced with great challenges en route to the Promised Land, God was quick to remind them of their past successes:

> You shall remember that you were a slave in the land of Egypt, and the Lord your God brought you out from there with a mighty hand and an outstretched arm (Deut. 5:15).

In the New Testament, Jesus instilled confidence in His disciples through vicarious experiences. He showed them how to exercise their faith and heal the sick. After Jesus went back to heaven, Peter and John were among those who performed great miracles because they watched Jesus do the same thing on numerous occasions.

The Word of God is full of verbal persuasion. King Solomon shared many nuggets of wisdom in relation to encouragement and affirmation:

> There is one whose rash words are like sword thrusts, but the tongue of the wise brings healing (Prov. 12:18).

But perhaps no better Scripture encapsulates this principle of confidence building than the one contained in the New Testament letter to the Hebrews:

> Let us hold on to the confession of our hope without wavering, for He who promised is faithful. And let us be concerned about one another in order to promote love and good works, not staying away from our worship meetings, as some habitually do, but encouraging each other, and all the more as you see the day drawing near (Heb. 10:23-25, *HCSB*).

As people who are trying to follow Christ, it is easy to lose confidence because we regularly miss the mark of how we ought to live our lives. In this passage, we receive some powerful advice on how we can gain, regain and remain confident.

1. We are told to "hold on to the confession of our hope without wavering," or in other words, we need to remember God's faithfulness and the source of our past successes.

2. We are advised to "be concerned about one another...not staying away from our worship meetings" in an effort to vicariously experience the successes of others.
3. We are challenged to "promote love and good works" and to verbally encourage each other.

We have all the tools we need to help our athletes become the confident young people God created them to be. We also have been given timeless instruction that will allow us to expand our influence as coaches well beyond the short time that we have with each of these kids who enter into our lives through the avenue of sports.

As Vince Lombardi said, "Confidence is contagious." It's time for us as coaches to create that environment of confidence within our teams in an effort to shape the direction of future generations.

Famous former USC football coach John Robinson has another interesting philosophy on confidence:

I never criticize a player until they are first convinced of my unconditional confidence in their abilities.

In other words, a player who knows he has the confidence of his coaches will always take criticism better. Being critical isn't inherently a negative trait. Being critical with no affirmation will kill the confident mindset, but criticism that comes from a foundation of genuine love and concern is much more likely to be received and processed in a positive manner.

Reaching the High Point

During the 2013 season at South Lake High School, I coached a senior receiver who was starting for the first time. Darius was a pretty good athlete. He had good hands and decent speed, but he had struggled in previous years due to some eligibility issues. Darius wasn't a belligerent kid. He wasn't lazy. He just struggled in the classroom and didn't have the best support system at home.

So when the new coaching staff came in, they took a lot of time working with his academics. Then over the summer break, we all went to an FCA camp. I immediately noticed that when he was just playing around, he was making some great catches. It was incredible to see how easily he performed when no one was really paying attention.

That's when I realized something important about Darius. Up to that point, his whole life had been built on a negative thought: *I'm a failure.* Because of that draining mindset, he needed more than anything to have his confidence restored. So I started coaching him that way.

Darius was a great Pop Warner player. Everybody would say, "You should have seen him play Pop Warner! He was incredible!" Well, no one had seen him play in three years because he had yet to be eligible to play at the high school level. The kid hadn't played since eighth grade!

"Darius, I heard you were awesome when you played Pop Warner!" I told him one day before practice.

I could see his shoulders lift and his back straighten up. Just a few encouraging words made an immediate difference in Darius's demeanor. During practice that day, he started making some great catches.

"Man, that's awesome how you got up and caught that ball!" I'd say. "You go to the high point. You're one of the few guys who knows how to catch the ball at the high point."

By the eighth game of the year, Darius had become our second leading receiver. The program was trying to make the playoffs after

10 losing seasons and his elevated play was a key part of whether the team would be successful or not.

Darius was very quiet. He didn't say much. But during the pre-game warm-ups, he came up to me, put his arm around me and said, "Coach, I love you."

That's all he said.

"Man, Darius, I love you," I replied. "Thank you."

Darius's story certainly speaks to motivation. The coaching staff stepped into his life and motivated him to improve his academic performance. But it was the next part of the process—restoring his confidence—that helped him reach his fullest potential on the field. Because we reminded him of his past successes and consistently showered him with positive reinforcement, Darius felt like he could do *anything* well.

And he ultimately reciprocated the love we all felt for him as a valued young man. I loved coaching Darius.

TRAINING TIME

1. Can you think of a time when a lack of confidence negatively impacted the performance of one of your athletes?
2. In this chapter we talked about performance accomplishments. What are some ways that you can document success stories in order to remind your athletes of past successes as related to performance in the future?
3. What are some ways that you have been or can begin using vicarious experiences to build confidence in your athletes?
4. What are some ways that you have been or can begin creating an atmosphere of encouragement for your team? How do you think encouragement will change the confidence level of your players?

5. How can you hold yourself, your coaches and your players accountable to build up and not tear down other athletes on your team or the opposing team?

PRAYER

Lord, help me to be an encourager and not a discourager. Give me the wisdom to restore my athletes to a place of confidence. Allow my words and my actions to serve as healing agents in their lives so that they might see the potential and purpose that You have placed inside of each one of them.

11

JOY!

After more than 30 years of coaching, I *still* love the passion of the game. I feel no different than during my first year in the profession when I was eager to take on multiple challenges with four teams in one year. As you might recall, my wife of one year compelled me to narrow that number down to one sport.

"This is crazy!" she said.

And it was a little bit crazy, but it was a lot of fun too.

I remember riding on the school bus to a JV basketball game that first year. There's nothing like being on a bus for an hour with a bunch of 14-year-old boys. Before long, they started to get rowdy and the noise rose to an unbearable level. So I did what any coach would do. I stood up, blew my whistle, and yelled at them.

"You all shut up, sit down and get your mind on the game!"

In that situation, I suppose two out of three isn't bad. They did shut up and they did sit down, but they only did those things because I was the coach. I'm pretty sure, however, that they didn't get their minds on the game. Truthfully, I just didn't understand their emotions. This is likely a problem for many of us coaches today, and this often leads us to make mistakes when dealing with our athletes.

To make matters more complicated, competitive athletics have the ability to put on display the whole range of human emotions. The thrill of victory, the agony of defeat, and everything in between is regularly felt on fields across the nation and around the world.

It can be a daunting proposition for those of us who signed up to be coaches, not psychologists.

The Emotion Matrix

Plain and simple, emotion is a response to something that's going on deeper inside an individual. For the athlete, emotion is usually a response to performance. Because sports are so closely tied to performance, there is a constant flow of emotions coming out of our athletes. Those emotions ultimately influence sports functioning and manifest in three definitive ways:

1. Physiologically (laughing, crying, etc.)
2. Psychologically (losing focus, losing motivation, etc.)
3. Behaviorally (pouting, ranting, giving up, etc.)

All emotions fit into two basic categories:

Pleasant (Positive)

- Excitement
- Joy
- Exhilaration

Unpleasant (Negative)

- Frustration
- Anger
- Fear
- Disappointment

Some emotions enhance performance while other emotions hinder performance. It's not as simple as just saying that some emotions are good and some emotions are bad. In fact, some pleasant emotions can be harmful (pleasant-harmful) while some unpleasant emotions can be helpful (unpleasant-helpful).

To help understand, we've created the Emotion Matrix.

The Emotion Matrix
- Pleasant-Helpful
- Pleasant-Harmful
- Unpleasant-Helpful
- Unpleasant-Harmful

In this chapter, we're going to focus on pleasant emotions and determine which ones are helpful and which ones are harmful.

Pleasant-Helpful
There are certain pleasant emotions that always help performance. These emotions should be cultivated and encouraged. Some of these emotions include:

- Excitement
- Joy
- Exhilaration

When these emotions manifest within your athletes and your team, you will see real results exhibited:

- Motivation—Athletes develop an internal drive that pushes them through adversity.
- Goal pursuit—Athletes look beyond the moment and see the big picture more clearly.

- Increased confidence—Athletes are no longer afraid of failure and become more willing to try new skills.
- Intensity regulation—Athletes are less likely to have negative emotional blow-ups during practice or during competition.
- Directed focus—Athletes become acutely aware of the task at hand.

Pleasant-Harmful

On the other hand, there are certain pleasant emotions that are actually harmful and hinder performance. These emotions should be quickly cut off and consistently discouraged:

- Satisfaction
- Complacency

Some of the harmful effects of these pleasant emotions include:

- Sense of completion—Athletes feel as if there is nothing left to accomplish and subsequently become unmotivated.
- Reduced intensity—Athletes lose interest in what they are doing and are no longer primed for optimal performance.
- Unfocused—Athletes become more easily distracted by outside interests that might present a new challenge.

Joy Robbers

In many ways, these pleasant emotions (both helpful and harmful) work against each other. Unfortunately, today's coaching culture can often be its own worst enemy. By its very nature, first-dimension coaching systematically removes the pleasant-helpful emotions from sports and unknowingly opens the door to a host of pleasant-harmful emotions.

For instance, let's take a closer look at the pleasant-helpful emotion of joy. First-dimension coaches have accepted that joy really doesn't have a place in sports. I was the same way early in my coaching career. I used to interpret joy as a lack of focus. And that meant loss of control. Coaches are all about control. We *need* to be in control.

Just like on the JV basketball team bus, my first inclination was to suppress that joy. And after a while, athletes will learn to suppress it too. And when they suppress joy, they aren't free to be who they were created to be. Ultimately, that means they aren't able to perform to their fullest potential.

||||||||||||||||||||||||||||||||||||||||||||||||||||||||||||||||||||||||||||||||||||||||

The National Counsel for Accreditation of Coaching says that at least 50 percent of coaching is an art.

||||||||||||||||||||||||||||||||||||||||||||||||||||||||||||||||||||||||||||||||||||||||

Coaching is an art because it's about creation. We were created in God's image, and according to Genesis 1:1, God was a Creator. We naturally get joy when we create. Coaches who allow kids to create within the context of sports will see freedom turn into joy, and joy will turn into great attitude and effort, and that great attitude and effort will turn into excellent performance.

But when we don't understand this, we instead replace our coaching with first-dimension concepts and phrases like, "Pick up your intensity!" or "We've got to outwork our opponent!"

As I've studied the difference between first-dimension coaching and second-dimension coaching, I've come to the conclusion that the teams that succeed are the ones that don't *outwork* their opponents, but rather *outplay* them.

Think back for a moment to when you were a kid. Think about those times when you were free to enjoy yourself. For most of us, it was being told by our parents to go spend the afternoon outside of the house. We played home run derby. We played Wiffle ball. We played tag. We played hide and seek. We played games for hours and didn't stop until the sun went down.

During those moments, we fully embraced the spirit of play, and our attitude and effort were outstanding! But now as coaches, we tell our athletes things like this: "We're going out to the practice field and do drills!"

I don't know about you, but when I hear the word "drill," I'm reminded of sitting in the waiting room at the dentist's office and hearing the awful buzzing sound of drills. I don't recall experiencing much joy during those visits.

Coaches, we have bought into a lie. We have come to believe that in order to become successful in sports, we have to work harder than the other guys. It's no longer about having fun. Work is something we do to pay the bills.

||||||||||||||||||||||||||||||||||||||||||||||||||||||||||||||||||||||||||||||||||||||||||||||||||||||||

Sports weren't meant to be work. Sports were meant to be play.

||||||||||||||||||||||||||||||||||||||||||||||||||||||||||||||||||||||||||||||||||||||||||||||||||||||||

This culture of work has done two very damaging things to sports. First, it has robbed sports of its joy. Second, it has taken the fun out of sports and replaced it with the pleasant-harmful emotion of complacency. There are two very simple solutions to these problems:

1. *Identify the joy robbers on your team.* Is it one of your coaches? Is it you? This may be the hardest thing to do in the

second dimension, but the joy robbers on your team have to change or they need to leave. When the joy robbers are gone, your team will be reinvigorated.

2. *Do away with the "outwork" mentality.* This will only lead to burnout for you, your coaches and especially your players, who will become complacent as they begin to realize that they can never truly work hard enough. Turning work into play will revolutionize your practices and produce better, more sustainable results on the field of play.

Before we go any further, let me make sure to answer the question that many are probably asking right about now: "How can our team be good if we don't put in the work and the effort to teach and practice the necessary skills?"

This simple answer to that question is, "You *can't* be good if you don't put in the work." That's why the key to this cyclical problem is *balance*. We must find the balance between work and play so that we can coach the athletes what they need to learn while retaining a sense of joy and fun that pushes back the emotions of complacency and satisfaction. Let's look at some creative things a few coaches have done.

Bringing Back the Joy

The Touchdown Celebration

In 2007, I was one of the speakers at the NIKE Coach of the Year Clinic. Georgia head football coach Mark Richt was the keynote speaker. As I took my turn on stage, I noticed that Coach Richt was taking a lot of notes. After the event concluded, he talked to me about his frustration with not being able to beat one of the team's biggest rivals, the Florida Gators. In fact, to that point, Georgia had only defeated Florida three times in the previous 18 seasons.

"I finally got it!" Richt said. "My team is always tight in the big games because we've focused on outworking our opponents. Our kids don't have any joy!"

As Georgia approached its annual game against Florida the following October, Richt encouraged his team to get excited when they scored a touchdown. He wanted it to be a team celebration that would hopefully instill some fun back into the game, just like being on a playground.

Richt didn't have to wait long to see how his team would react. The Bulldogs took the opening drive down the field for a touchdown. The team erupted as Knowshon Moreno crossed the goal line. Over 70 players ran to the end zone for a first quarter celebration like no one had seen before. Needless to say, every single official threw penalty flags until there were 10 yellow hankies strewn all over the field.

The following week, Richt sent a letter of apology to the Southeastern Conference for the outburst. His intent was to have the 11 men on the field celebrate collectively in the end zone. Richt hadn't taken into account that his entire squad would join in the celebration. But the greater impact was still intact. According to Richt, his players gave an outstanding effort and played much better—a result that he unequivocally attributed to the team's renewed sense of joy.

Tag! You're It!

Here's a question for you basketball coaches: When was the last time a player came to you before practice and eagerly asked how many suicides you were going to make the team run? My guess is never.

Well, here's one story that a high school basketball coach told me. His team was a perennial 6A contender, despite the fact that he rarely if ever had any kids who were taller than 5'11". The team was especially good on defense. The players had to be in great shape because of their non-stop hustle that stretched opponents from baseline to baseline.

In order to maintain the team's conditioning, the coach was disciplined in his regimen of cardio workouts, such as line drills (or suicides, as they are often called). The kids hated it. It was like going to work. There was nothing fun about those practices.

The coach knew he needed to come up with something different to keep his athletes from becoming complacent. One day he was thinking back to his childhood and his annual trip to the family reunion. His grandmother's house was located on a busy street in the city, so they had to stay within the picket fence. This coach specifically remembered how he and the other kids relentlessly played tag out in the front yard while the adults sat around talking in the house.

That was it. He had his solution. He was going to bring the playground to the practice court.

At the next practice, he gathered his 15 players together in a huddle. He pointed at three of the boys and said, "You three kids are it. The only rule is that you have to stay on the basketball court. If you get tagged, you have to run line drills with me on the sidelines."

The coach blew his whistle and off they went. They didn't need any further instruction. The players were back peddling, sidestepping, twisting and twirling. It turned out to be some of the best cardio training he had ever conducted.

After several minutes of chaotic fun, he pulled the players back together. They were sweating profusely. They were bent over with their hands on their knees. Their heart rates were through the roof. And most important, as they lifted their heads to give the coach their attention, they all had big smiles on their faces.

The team now plays tag every day in practice. The coach now breaks it down by position. He puts the low post players together, the wings together and the guards together. Not one day goes by when one of his athletes doesn't ask before practice, "We're playing tag today, aren't we?" When was the last time a player blurted out with a smile, "We're doing bunches of suicides today aren't we, Coach?"

Upside-Down Practice

It doesn't take long into the season before football practice can become very mundane. That was the experience we had at East Ridge. The coaching staff decided to come up with a fun exercise to help make practice a little more interesting. We created what we called "upside-down practice."

At the end of each practice, we put the ball on the 10-yard line. The skilled offensive players traded places with the offensive line. The quarterback played guard. The center played running back—or whatever variation the athletes chose. The same went for the defensive side of the ball. Cornerbacks became defensive linemen and tackles had to guard the receivers.

It only took about two minutes of practice, but we quickly noticed that our players gave a better effort for the entire session if they knew they were going to get four upside-down plays. This simple but creative method elevated the team's practices. The team gave a collective, more sustained effort and maintained a great attitude throughout. Plus, it was just a lot of fun to watch! Why? The linemen who never get to touch the football get to in this game—just like on the playground. Nobody ever went to the playground as a kid and volunteered to be a lineman. Every kid wants to touch the ball and score. So let them!

Charles Schaefer had it right when he made this astute observation:

We are never more fully alive, more completely ourselves or more deeply engrossed in anything, than when we are at play.

Doing these things is not a waste of time. It is, in fact, essential that we create opportunities for joy to come out of our athletes. Not only will it change our players, but it will also bring the passion back to our coaching.

An Atmosphere of Joy

During His ministry on Earth, there's no question that Jesus worked hard. He walked from town to town on foot and spent hours teaching the masses and healing the sick. But Jesus understood better than anyone that joy was the emotion that most needed to be enhanced—especially in the lives of His team members.

That's why Jesus spent time alone with the disciples. They got away from the crowds and relaxed in people's homes, at their campsites, and out on the sea in their boat. Jesus demonstrated that it was okay to rejoice and to have fun. He did this by publicly entertaining the children who were drawn to Him (see Matt. 19:13-15). He also did it by outwardly expressing joy when others received a revelation from God (see Luke 10:21). At times, Jesus was even accused of being *too* joyful by the Pharisees, who accused Him of being "a glutton and a drunkard" and "a friend of tax collectors and sinners" (Luke 7:34).

Just as He taught His disciples, so too Jesus wants us to experience joy in our journey. That is equally true for coaches and for their athletes. Again, this doesn't mean we are to do away with hard work and effort. It also doesn't mean we will never experience negative emotions like pain and hurt.

But joy is deeper than that. Joy is something that comes out of our inner being. It's something that can overcome even the darkest moments in our lives. As the prophet Nehemiah wrote, "The joy of the Lord is your strength" (Neh. 8:10).

Jesus explained it to His team this way:

> If you keep my commands, you will remain in my love, just as I have kept my Father's commands and remain in His love. I have told you this so that my joy may be in you and that your joy may be complete (John 15:10-11).

When you love what you do, you will discover unshakable joy. Jesus described that kind of joy as being "complete." Joy, in the perfect sense, is wrapped around the concept of love. Joy always produces great attitude and effort, whereas the performance-driven mindset or work creates burnout and complacency.

Jesus taught His disciples to diligently pursue their mission with a joyful attitude. He didn't want them to follow His lead out of a sense of obligation, but rather because they had a sense of excitement and expectation based on their love for God. Jesus knew He was going to face the unthinkable. He knew He was going to be tortured, whipped, beaten and hung on a cross as a sacrifice for the sins of the world. Yet along that road—the road to the cross—He maintained His joy.

||||||||||||||||||||||||||||||||||||||||||||||||||||||||||||||||||||||||||||||||||||||||||||||||||

Joy can motivate us even in those times
when the external reasons to keep going
seem to have disappeared.

||||||||||||||||||||||||||||||||||||||||||||||||||||||||||||||||||||||||||||||||||||||||||||||||||

Jesus also knew that His team would face great difficulties in the near future. They would do great things in His name, but they would ultimately face great persecution because of their faith in God. The apostle Paul, who was converted to the Christian faith after a miraculous encounter with Jesus, wrote these words that so eloquently capture the power of joy in the lives of those who choose to embrace it:

> Therefore, since we also have such a large cloud of witnesses surrounding us, let us lay aside every weight and the sin that so easily ensnares us. Let us run with endurance the race that lies before us, keeping our eyes on Jesus, the source and perfecter of our faith, who for the joy that lay before Him endured a cross and despised the shame and has sat down at the right hand of God's throne (Heb. 12:1-12).

The first dimension and the second dimension are intricately connected. Joy is a second-dimension attribute that can drastically impact attitude and effort toward first-dimension objectives. When joy is present, athletes will gladly endure vigorous training regimens and countless hours of work.

The same is true for those of us who embark on a life-changing journey as followers of Jesus Christ. When we truly love Him, we will joyfully walk out our faith, no matter what challenges might come our way.

TRAINING TIME

1. Identify a time when emotions positively impacted your ability to coach at a high level? What about a time when emotions negatively impacted you as a coach?

2. What are some pleasant-helpful emotions that you have seen enhance athletic performance? What are some pleasant-harmful emotions that have negatively impacted your team?
3. How have you personally struggled with the balance between the concepts of work and play? Explain.
4. Are you able to identify some of the joy robbers on your team? How have they negatively impacted your team? What can you do to limit or eliminate the joy robbing that take places within your team?
5. What are some new ways you can bring joy to your team?

PRAYER

Lord, help me to rediscover the joy of the game through play. Help me to identify and get rid of the joy robbers that are negatively impacting my athletes. Help me to daily remember that Your joy is my strength. Give me the strength to resist the harmful emotions of satisfaction and complacency, both as a coach and as a follower of Christ.

12

ANGER MANAGEMENT

I coached at Florida State with Bobby Bowden for three years. In that time, I heard him cuss only three times. It was the same word all three times and one that would be considered mild by today's standards.

On one occasion, the team was having a bad practice. Some of the players had shown up late and the overall attitude just wasn't very good. After one athlete gave a particularly poor effort on a play, Coach Bowden grabbed him by the arm and swore at him. Everyone looked up. They knew Coach meant business. Although I'm sure he wasn't proud of the outburst, it was certainly effective, considering the circumstances.

> Anybody can become angry—that is easy, but to be angry with the right person and to the right degree and at the right time and for the right purpose, and in the right way—that is not within everybody's power and is not easy. —Aristotle

So why do so many coaches curse? That's a question I've often pondered during my 30-plus years in the business. My conclusion? I believe that the coaches who curse do so because they don't know how to do things out of joy. They only know how to express frustration in anger.

Eventually, the cursing becomes ineffective, so they have to keep adding new curse words. It would be comical if it weren't so sad.

The language on our fields and courts has become tremendously bad over the past two or three generations. Can you imagine a science teacher talking that way to his or her students? Why do we coaches think we have the right to talk that way to our athletes?

The good news is, it's possible to change. It should be the goal of every coach to help athletes gain mastery over their emotions so that they can help rather than harm athletic performance. It begins with a coach's personal awareness of the emotional response and its effects, and then by helping the athlete become aware, take control and practice responding accordingly. But before that can happen, the coach must have control over his or her *own* emotions.

Anger isn't the only emotion we will discuss in this chapter, but it's one of the most complex. Paraphrasing the great philosopher Aristotle's words: Anger can be both helpful and harmful depending on the circumstances. But knowing the difference "is not easy."

Unpleasant Emotions

As we discussed in the last chapter, emotion is a response to performance. This physiological truth manifests itself nowhere more clearly than in the sports culture. To better explain the varying effects of pleasant and unpleasant emotions (both helpful and harmful), let's take another look at the Emotion Matrix.

The Emotion Matrix

- Pleasant-Helpful
- Pleasant-Harmful
- Unpleasant-Helpful
- Unpleasant-Harmful

In the last chapter, we looked at pleasant emotions. In this chapter, we're going to discuss unpleasant emotions.

Unpleasant-Helpful

It might seem contrary to our human logic, but there are certain unpleasant emotions that actually help performance. Sports create moments when things don't work out well. That's when these emotions can serve as powerful coaching tools:

- Short-term frustration
- Short-term anger
- Short-term disappointment

"Short-term" is the key. When something has been done wrong that hurts the whole team or perhaps when there has been an injustice, it's okay to show short-term anger, short-term frustration or short-term disappointment in an effort to swiftly correct the problem and to help the offending party make a positive change in behavior. But once it's over, it needs to be over for good. Get it done and then get back to coaching.

Used correctly, unpleasant-helpful emotions can bring forth a variety of positive results:

- Motivation—An impetus to clear obstacles is triggered within athletes.
- Increased confidence—Athletes are lifted to new levels of belief and self-assurance.
- Elevation of intensity—Athletes are pushed out of their comfort zone and into a higher level of emotional involvement.
- Distraction from pain—Athletes who are injured can focus their mind away from a distressed physical circumstance.

Unpleasant-Harmful

On the other hand, there are many unpleasant emotions that are simply harmful and hinder performance. As you can imagine, the list is lengthy and contains emotions to which we can all relate:

- Fear
- Desperation
- Panic
- Guilt
- Embarrassment
- Shame
- Distress
- Sadness
- Rage

Some of the harmful effects of these unpleasant emotions include:

- Unhealthy levels of intensity—This hinders execution as athletes get too ramped up and begin to tighten up on the field of play.
- Physical and psychological shutdown—Athletes can no longer handle the pressure. They become physically and/or mentally unable to perform important skills and tasks.

While many of those harmful emotions find their way into today's coaching landscape, there are two in particular that stand out: shame and embarrassment.

They usually go hand in hand. Public humiliation is, unfortunately, the standard operating procedure for coaches who don't understand how to get better results with positive reinforcement. It actually might work for a while. It might cause the player to rise up and play with some anger. Or it might have the opposite effect and cause the player to shut down under the weight of disgrace and indignity.

We have a stark picture of how these harmful emotions impacted the Master Coach in three different Gospel accounts. Jesus had gone to the Mount of Olives and a place commonly referred to as the Garden of Gethsemane. There He gathered with His disciples and prayed late into the night. He knew that His time on earth was nearing an end. Jesus was soon to lay down His life for the sins of the world.

Think about it. Jesus told the disciples in Matthew 26:38, "My soul is overwhelmed with sorrow to the point of death." He knew He would have to carry the shame and embarrassment that accompanied the sins of an entire planet. Jesus knew that His own Father would reject Him while He was dying on the cross. According to the account in Luke 22:44, "His sweat was like drops of blood falling to the ground."

"Abba, Father," He cried out to God, "everything is possible for You. Take this cup from me" (Mark 14:36).

If Jesus, the Son of God, almost shut down under the pressure of immense shame, how do you think a 16-year-old kid is going to respond when embarrassed by an unapologetic coach? Yet that's what I used to do. That's what so many coaches still do today. And why? Is it because he doesn't run fast enough or hustle enough? Does that mean he's lazy? Well, maybe he's tired. Or maybe he's bored to death and hates being out there. Maybe I need to be a coach and have a strategy that allows joy to be expressed. *That* is coaching in the second dimension.

Sadly, the modern sports culture is inundated with embarrassment, shame and other harmful emotions. It has become commonplace to hear about coaches who are walking a thin line and sometimes even crossing over into abusive behavior—all in the name of pushing athletes to a higher level of performance.

But if we want to elevate ourselves above this destructive manifestation and become 3D Coaches, we must reject the use of harmful emotions and do everything we can to create a counter culture that has its foundation in peace, joy and love.

Anger Management

It's okay to get angry if it's short-term and doesn't have long-term repercussions. We've seen how short-term anger can be an effective coaching method as demonstrated in the legendary career of notable 3D Coaches such as the aforementioned Bobby Bowden and the late Hall of Fame basketball coach John Wooden.

But if you're still not convinced, let's take a look at the Master Coach and see how *He* utilized short-term anger:

> When it was almost time for the Jewish Passover, Jesus went up to Jerusalem. In the temple courts he found people selling cattle, sheep and doves, and others sitting at tables exchanging money. So he made a whip out of cords, and drove all from the temple courts, both sheep and cattle; he scattered the coins of the moneychangers and overturned their tables. To those who sold doves he said, "Get these out of here! Stop turning my Father's house into a market!" (John 2:13-16).

When someone has done something wrong—morally or ethically—it's okay to get angry. When someone's rights have been violated, that's when you might need to step in and make a statement. That's what Jesus was doing in the temple. The people had turned a house of worship into a market. This angered Jesus and He proceeded to make a scene. He raised His voice. He turned over the Gatorade table.

But once Jesus had made His point, He went back to teaching. One of the Gospels tells us that "The blind and the lame came to Him at the temple, and He healed them" (Matt. 21:14). In other words, Jesus continued to show love and compassion for those who most needed His attention—even in the wake of His righteous romp.

On a practical level, anger loses its effectiveness once it wears out its welcome, or worse, when it crosses over into rage. That's when athletes begin to shut down and respond with negative emotions.

On a spiritual level, long-term anger opens the heart up to temptation. It allows unhealthy emotions such as bitterness, unforgiveness and pride to set up shop within our flesh. The apostle Paul strongly warns against this in his letter to the church in Ephesus:

> In your anger do not sin: Do not let the sun go down while you are still angry, and do not give the devil a foothold (Eph. 4:26-27).

Paul also addresses this concept indirectly in one of his letters to the church in Corinth:

> Everything is permissible, but not everything is helpful. Everything is permissible, but not everything builds up. No one should seek his own good, but the good of the other person (1 Cor. 10:23-24, *HCSB*).

Paul is actually addressing a question about what Christians should and shouldn't eat. There was a controversy at the time regarding food that had been sacrificed to idols. Was it unholy to consume? But Paul broadened the question to include anything that may or may not have been acceptable within the Jewish culture from which most of the early Christians had emerged. Instead of making it about right versus wrong, Paul connected all of these issues to the bigger picture. "No one should seek his own good," he wrote, "but for the good of the other person."

So even if you deem that unpleasant emotions such as short-term anger or short-term frustration might work within the context of correcting or motivating your players, those tactics should always be based in godly love for them and should never be driven by selfish intentions.

The Fruits of Spirit-led Coaching

Perhaps you've found yourself struggling to find balance in your use of unpleasant-helpful emotions. Or maybe you've been fighting the temptation to yield to your flesh and turn to unpleasant-harmful emotions as a quick fix for the motivational or behavioral problems on your team.

No matter the situation, you can lean on God's Word for the answer to what it looks like to be a 3D Coach dealing with the emotions of your athletes:

> But the fruit of the Spirit is love, joy, peace, patience, kindness, goodness, faithfulness, gentleness, self-control; against such things there is no law. And those who belong to Christ Jesus have crucified the flesh with its passions and desires. If we live by the Spirit, let us also walk by the Spirit (Gal. 5:22-25, HCSB).

If your use of anger and frustration is producing motivation, confidence and healthy intensity within your athletes, chances are you are living and walking by the Spirit. But if your athletes are reaching unhealthy levels of intensity or, conversely, shutting down on you, it might be time to take a closer look at Paul's letter to the Galatians.

When anger drags on into the long-term, it means it's becoming less about godly love and more about selfish pride. When frustration gravitates towards shame and embarrassment, it means that your coaching isn't being led by the Spirit, but rather by the flesh.

Emotions are a powerful part of the human experience—especially within the sports culture where performance is often the driving force. A 3D Coach will allow the Spirit to show him the correct and most effective ways to harness the helpful emotions and get rid of the harmful ones. The fruit will be evident to everyone within that circle of influence and beyond.

TRAINING TIME

1. Think back to your days as an athlete. What is the most passionate display of emotions you have ever witnessed from one of your coaches? Can you share a story where you showed intense emotion to an athlete or to your team?
2. What are some things that can cause you to become angry or frustrated as a coach?
3. Were you ever shamed or embarrassed by one of your coaches? How did that affect you?
4. Read Galatians 5:22-25. Which of the fruits of the Spirit do you struggle to demonstrate in your coaching? How do you think the

atmosphere around your program would change if you were able to consistently coach with these attributes in mind?

5. What are some strategies that you can implement to help yourself stay under control when you are tempted to display unpleasant-harmful emotions, such as anger and shame?

PRAYER

Lord, help me to discern between unpleasant-helpful emotions and unpleasant-harmful emotions. Help me to wisely use anger and frustration as short-term methods of correction and training, and only if it can be done with a pure sense of love and compassion for my athletes. Deliver me from the temptation to use harmful emotions in any way, shape or form. I want to walk by Your Spirit. I want to influence others for Your Kingdom. I want my coaching to bring glory to Your name.

13

IN THE SPOTLIGHT

Tony Dungy isn't an NFL legend because of his brief playing career. He is a highly respected man within the sport due to the notable leadership skills he displayed as head coach of the Tampa Bay Buccaneers and the Indianapolis Colts. But in three years, Dungy learned some valuable lessons about team cohesion that he would carry throughout the next 20-plus years of his professional life.

More specifically, Dungy picked up on some important principles while spending two years playing with the Pittsburgh Steelers (1977–1978) and later working as an assistant coach for that same team (1981–1988).

When Dungy showed up for training camp prior to the 1977 season, the quarterback turned defensive back was initially overwhelmed by his surroundings. Pittsburgh was on the verge of becoming a dynasty with four Super Bowl championships in six years. The team featured 10 future Pro Football Hall of Fame inductees, including Terry Bradshaw, Franco Harris, Lynn Swann, "Mean" Joe Greene and Jack Lambert.

Like most outsiders, Dungy initially assumed that it was the team's star power that served as the main ingredient for success. But the young rookie quickly found out it was something much different.

"It was the practices," Dungy once said. "It was everybody working together. It was the offensive guys helping the defensive guys. It was the close-knit nature of the team that made us hard to beat much more so than just the individual star players."[1]

Dungy credits head coach Chuck Noll with setting the tone. It was from Noll's example that Dungy was able to take that concept and achieve similar results in his 12-year head-coaching career. Towards the end of his NFL coaching career, he made this powerful statement:

The enemy of teamwork is individualism. As a team, the whole has to be greater than the sum of every individual part. The only way to do that is to work together. You can go a lot farther pulling together than you can with individual people pulling separately.[2]

Sadly, that pluralistic culture has been tragically muted by the entitlement culture that has engulfed our society and bled deeply into the world of sports. On the other hand, it's a beautiful thing when a team becomes unified in pursuit of a goal. We as coaches know it when we see it. Team chemistry has a palpable look and feel. But how can we teach it to emerging generations of athletes who struggle with the concept of "we" in a "me"-centered environment?

Let's take a look at some of the social dynamics that contribute to the problem and then start unpacking some practical solutions that will revolutionize the way your team works together.

Team Cohesion

It's funny how it goes sometimes. The best teams aren't always made up of the best players. A team that has the most talented athletes might not reach its full potential. The Michigan University men's basketball team from 1991–1993 provides one of the best examples of this reality. Chris Webber, Juwan Howard, Jalen Rose, Jimmy King and Ray Jackson made up one of the best recruiting classes in NCAA history. Yet all of that star power could not produce a national championship. The vaunted "Fab Five" lost consecutive title games to Duke (1992) and North Carolina (1993) before its nucleus was sifted by the NBA Draft.

On the other hand, a group of average athletes can often come together to become one of the *best* teams. The 1980 U.S. Olympic Hockey team serves as one of the most powerful examples of this phenomenon. According to the experts, there was virtually no way the seventh-seeded team could win that tournament or even win a medal. Yet head coach Herb Brooks used second-dimension principles to inspire a group of overachieving athletes to upset the Russians in the semifinal game, 4-3, and then defeat Finland, 4-2, to win the gold medal.

In some cases, a team's failure to succeed has nothing to do with its ability or inability to work together as a single-minded unit. Sometimes the other team just performs better. But in many cases, talented teams fall short due to a lack of team chemistry while less-talented teams overachieve because of strong team chemistry.

We like to refer to it as Team Cohesion. It's when a group of individuals bond at a relational level and therefore create a sense of unity and loyalty that is not easily shaken. So how do we get our teams to that level? First, we need to break down the dynamics of the team unit and how they are coached.

Individuals vs. the Group

As a coach, you are daily required to interact with two segments within the team. You deal with individual players in one-on-one settings, and you deal with the entire group as a whole. Here's how that typically looks:

- *Individuals*: You focus on the particular concerns of individual team members. You consider the roles and responsibilities of team members and their feelings about their place on the team.
- *The Group*: You place emphasis on the functions of the team without regard to the concerns of its individual members. You work to obtain team unity towards a common goal.

Task vs. Relational

According to Dr. Albert Carron, a professor at the University of Western Ontario and foremost expert on team cohesion, there are also two different ways that you can coach those two components of the team. Sometimes you utilize tasks and other times you rely on relational methods. For instance:

1. *Task*: Team members perform to a measured (usually physical) goal using traditional techniques such as practice drills or team scrimmages. This is a first-dimension concept.
2. *Relational*: Coaches show a greater concern for social relationships within the team and how every member fits into the team relationally. This is a second-dimension concept.

When you put it all together, you have four unique opportunities to impact team cohesion as a coach:

1. *Individual Task*: This is the extent to which the individual's actions are coordinated with the group's actions in order

to achieve its goals. Every practice has first-dimension individual drills. In football we call this practice time "indy" (short for individual). This includes time to block, tackle, run, pass and catch.

2. *Group Task*: This is the way the group functions as a whole to achieve its goals. In football, we call this "group" time. This includes the seven-on-seven, o-line versus d-line, and scrimmage.

3. *Individual Relational*: This is the quality of the individual members' relationships within the team.

4. *Group Relational*: This is the general quality of the relationship in the group.

Of the key second-dimension components, team cohesion is my favorite. It's what led me to meet with Dr. Carron and study it even further. What I learned is that you must have a strategy in all four areas that impact team cohesion. Having a consistent plan will help you take those talented teams and make them even better. A team cohesion strategy will also help you take those teams full of mediocre talent and turn them into a group of overachievers.

For the purposes of this conversation, we aren't going to focus on individual-task or group-task concepts. Those are first-dimension concepts that all quality coaches use. If you're struggling in those areas, there are plenty of resources available to help you improve at the task levels.

But to truly become great, you have to introduce the relational component. In this chapter, we're going to look specifically at the individual-relational aspect of team cohesion. One of the best ways to improve the quality of the individual members' relationships within the team is to introduce something in your practice that allows everyone to learn more about each other.

Strategies for Team Cohesion

The Knight Time

Several years ago, our teams at East Ridge started doing something called the Knight Time or, as some people call it, the Spotlight Drill. At the end of every practice, we had the team make a circle and then we had one player stand in the middle. For the next few minutes, everyone on the team had to say one thing that the player brought to the team. But it couldn't be anything athletic. It had to go deeper than that.

At first, it can be very awkward. You're dealing with young people who haven't seen this modeled very often in our culture. Of course, some kids who are uncomfortable with the process might lean on humor or mild sarcasm: "Hey, Jimmy, you've got nice hair!"

But eventually, the concept takes root and you start to hear some pretty amazing things from your players:

"Hey, John, you don't get a lot of playing time during the games, but I really appreciate the hustle and effort you give during practices."

"Andrew, you have a great personality. You know how to make us laugh when things get a little too tense."

"Bradley, I know you're one of our star players, but I just wanted to say thanks for being such a good friend. You really do care about your teammates."

We saw the kids transform before our eyes. Why? Because many of them rarely had someone tell them why they're special. You'll be amazed how it impacts everyone on the team. Your scout team members will play harder in practice. Your role players will give a better effort in their limited time on the field or on the court. Your best athletes will be affirmed for non-athletic things. And new kids are more organically welcomed into the fold.

A few years ago, we were doing the Knight Time during spring practice. At that time we did it by positions. I was working with receivers and quarterbacks—a group that had about 12 kids. On the third day, I had to miss practice due to a speaking engagement. Upon returning, I ended the practice as usual, by calling the next person who was set to take center stage.

"T.O.! You're up!" I shouted.

A young man who resembled Terrell Owens (hence the nickname) stepped up and delivered some surprising news.

"No, Coach," he responded. "It's not my turn. I've already done it."

That's right. They did it on their own without me! Why? It's because they began to feel that someone valued them—and not for what they could do on the field but for who they were as people. Try it for a few days and then "forget" to do it one day. Just see what happens. They'll beg for it! "Coach! Don't forget the Knight Time drill!"

But here's another amazing thing that happens. Think about the parents who hover around the practice field. We're always a little nervous about those parents. They always seem to have some advice for us or, worse, unresolved criticisms about our game planning or the way we utilize their child on the field.

So when you do an individual-relational activity like the Spotlight Drill, at the end of practice invite the parents to come and observe. It absolutely changes the way you are viewed as a coach. Nothing lights a parent's fire more than seeing their child publicly affirmed by others. Now, instead of sitting in the stands and badmouthing you to their friends, the hearts of those parents with a negative attitude are softened.

"Coach is awesome!"
"Coach really knows how to motivate these kids!"

Even if their kid is on the bench, they have seen a difference. They have seen you doing something in a higher dimension. And what mom or dad doesn't think their kid is special?

Helmet Stickers

Something we instituted at East Ridge that helped foster group-relational growth within the team was a twist on the concept of helmet stickers. Although many high school programs no longer allow helmet awards, our school maintained the tradition of hanging out helmet stickers to players who performed the best in each game.

Instead of recognizing the most valuable players on the field with first-dimension results (like blocks, tackles, receptions, interceptions and pass completions), we honored the athletes who did something to make the team better by serving someone else. And it wasn't coaches who handed out the stickers. It was the players who gave them away.

Over time, other programs picked up on what we were doing and began instituting their own take on this individual-relational program. A year ago, I was invited to sit in on one team's weekly helmet sticker event. It was all I could do to hold back the tears.

"Bobby, I want to give you a helmet award for giving Jack a ride home from practice."

"Coach, I saw Tyler, Joseph and D. J. helping the lunch lady clean up the cafeteria this week and I think they should all get helmet awards."

"Jake, I thought it was really cool when you stood up for that boy who was being teased in the hallway. You deserve a helmet award for that."

That Friday night, I went to the team's game and noticed something unusual. There were more kids on the bench with helmet stickers than the starters. The coach noticed the same thing we had observed with our team. The scout team began playing harder during practice and all of the players tended to give a more consistent effort because of the relationships that had been built throughout the program. In fact, we often had to cut practices short so the second team kids didn't kill our first team athletes with their effort as a scout team!

Those young men were more motivated because they had been affirmed. They felt like they were part of the team. This kind of cohesion goes way beyond individual or group tasks.

I think of former back-up slot receivers Matt Tebow and Brad Cox. Both are great young men who continue to live in the area. I've spoken to each in the years since they graduated high school and have been amazed at the life lessons they have learned from football and how those lessons have impacted them so strongly as adults. Remember, these players were back-ups and scout team players through their senior year, yet they genuinely loved their playing experience at East Ridge.

So what is *your* plan to bring your team together by using individual-relational activities?

Transforming the Team

When Coach Jesus interacted with His team, He used the same tools we use today, including first-dimension concepts such as the individual-task and group-task methods for creating team cohesion. For instance, Jesus gave His disciples an individual-task when He sent them to get the Upper Room ready for the Last Supper (see Mark 14:12-16). He also engaged His team in group-task when He allowed them to assist as He fed 5,000 hungry followers along the seashore (see Matt. 14:13-21).

But Jesus knew the real key to team cohesion was through relational interactions. He demonstrated this from the very beginning of His ministry as He recruited His team members.

> As He was walking along the Sea of Galilee, He saw two brothers, Simon, who was called Peter, and his brother Andrew. They were casting a net into the sea, since they were fishermen. "Follow Me," He told them, "and I will make you fish for people!" Immediately they left their nets and followed Him (Matt. 4:18, *HCSB*).

Jesus intentionally engaged the disciples and called them into a relationship with Himself. He didn't do this just for the purpose of having a private relationship; rather He did it to lay the foundation for what would eventually become a team made up of 12 men.

Matthew wrote about a time when, much later in Jesus' ministry, Jesus took three of His most trusted team members—Peter, James and John—up a high mountain where He was transfigured before them. Jesus, the Master Coach, was the first to initiate the concept of Captain's Camp, which is now a great part of FCA.

> His face shone like the sun, and His clothes became as white as the light. Just then there appeared before them Moses and Elijah, talking with Jesus (Matt. 17:2-3).

By allowing those men to see such a spectacular miracle, Jesus was deepening the process of transformation that He had begun the first day He invited those fishermen to follow Him. He revealed Himself in glory in an effort to transform the team. But it didn't take place overnight. It was a journey that would continue all the way until Jesus' death, resurrection and ascension.

In fact, Jesus was with His team for about three-and-a-half years. In that time, He diligently taught them the dangers of the "me"-centered mindset as well as the beauty and power of "we." The recurring theme was always built upon the divine concept of selfless love.

> I give you a new command: Love one another. Just as I have loved you, you must also love one another. By this all people will know that you are My disciples, if you have love for one another (John 13:34-35, *HCSB*).

Like Jesus, you get to be with each team for about three to four years. In the first dimension, you are responsible for implementing physical tasks that develop the individual *and* the team unit. But the team will never be truly whole if the individual relationships between the players are not based on selfless love and mutual respect for one another.

When your athletes have "love for one another," that is when you will know that the team has taken a big step from "me" to "we."

TRAINING TIME

1. How has the entitlement (me-centered) culture negatively impacted your ability to create team (we-centered) cohesion?

2. Have you ever coached a talented team that underachieved? Likewise, have you ever coached an average group of athletes that collectively overachieved? What was the difference between the two?
3. What are some things that you typically do in practice to coach using individual relational and group relational methods? Why are those elements important to the team?
4. What does it look like for athletes to "love one another"? Can you share some examples of how this has played out on your team?
5. The Knight Time drill and Helmet Awards are both great ways to foster better relationships between athletes. What are some other ideas that might garner similar results?

PRAYER

Lord, thank You for taking the time to care about my individual needs. Thank You for also inviting me to become a valued part of Your team. Help me to coach with that same attitude. Give me creative ways to connect the individuals within my team so that they might have true love and respect for one another and reflect the unity that You desire to see take place within Your Kingdom.

Notes

1. Fellowship of Christian Athletes, *Teamwork* (Ventura, CA: Regal Books, 2009), p. 23.
2. Ibid., p. 16.

14

FROM ME TO WE

John Wooden is arguably the greatest coach in the history of organized sports. The numbers are staggering. In his days at UCLA, the Bruins won an unprecedented 10 NCAA Men's Basketball National Championships including four teams that finished their seasons 30-0.

But Coach Wooden is known for so much more than his coaching career. Over time, he has become a national treasure thanks to his inspirational sayings and his iconic "Pyramid of Success," which teaches people from the sports world and beyond how to build the foundation for a meaningful life.

While many of Coach Wooden's teams were stacked with incredible talent, some of his teams consisted of overachieving athletes who put on impressive displays of teamwork en route to large-scale success.

||||||||||||||||||||||||||||||||||||||||||||||||||||||||||||||||||||||||||||||||||||||||||||||||||||||||||||||||||||

Regardless of what kind of players Coach Wooden had
on his teams, there was always one common thread.
His athletes were bonded together by something
much bigger than basketball.

||||||||||||||||||||||||||||||||||||||||||||||||||||||||||||||||||||||||||||||||||||||||||||||||||||||||||||||||||||

We always want to know if we can count on our teammates. When we know that they will be there to support us in tight spots, we are more likely to go the extra mile when they too need help. That combination makes each of us better. Loyalty is the force that forges individuals into a team. It's the component that moves teams toward great achievements.[1]

Perhaps better than anyone, Coach Wooden understood the importance of the individual-relational and group-relational concepts. From an individual-relational standpoint, he preached and modeled the value of acknowledging what each player brought to the team.

For instance, Coach Wooden encouraged his players to always give a gesture of thanks to other players for things like setting a good pick or making a great pass that led to a basket.

But it didn't stop there. Coach Wooden made sure that after every game—whether at home or on the road—his team cleaned up the locker room before they left the facility.

I don't believe a year ever went by when I didn't receive a letter from a custodian from one of the arenas where we played, indicating that we left the dressing room cleaner than anybody else.[2]

Through seemingly small things like acknowledging a teammates effort during competition or working together as a team to serve someone else, Coach Wooden knew that those were key moments in developing loyalty and moving the team "toward great achievements." He firmly knew from experience that nothing else brings a group of athletes together like these relational, team-building concepts.

The Relational Team

Everybody can be great because anybody can serve. You don't have to have a college degree to serve. You don't have to

make your subject and verb agree to serve. You only need a heart full of grace. A soul generated by love.
—Dr. Martin Luther King Jr.

What a powerful statement from one of the greatest servant leaders our world has ever known! Dr. King wasn't specifically talking about athletes, but his concept of serving others most certainly applies. It just so happens that serving is one of the most effective ways to build team cohesion at any level of sports. Athletes from youth leagues, junior high school, high school, college and the professional ranks can all greatly benefit when they first turn their efforts to others.

As a quick review of what we discussed in the previous chapter, team cohesion happens when a group of individuals bond at a relational level and create a strong sense of unity and loyalty. The four areas where team cohesion can be developed include:

1. *Individual Task*: This is the extent to which the individual's actions are coordinated with the group's actions in order to achieve its goals.
2. *Group Task*: This is the way the group functions as a whole to achieve its goals
3. *Individual Relational*: This is the quality of the individual members' relationships within the team.
4. *Group Relational*: This is the general quality of the relationship in the group.

In this chapter, we're going to keep our focus on the group-relational area.

One of the best ways to create unity is to give your athletes the opportunity to serve others. Even if it is just once a year, there's something special that takes place when a group comes together for a common goal that takes them outside of sports and introduces them to a higher purpose. This might be working with Habitat for Humanity to help build someone a home. It could be painting someone's house. It could be visiting a children's hospital. It could be serving meals to homeless families on Thanksgiving. There are countless ways that teams can come together to serve others within your community.

Another way to build team cohesion is to develop an action plan that lets the team enjoy each other's company away from the sports environment. It might be something as easy as having a meal together, or perhaps it could be something a little more involved like going to a ropes course or attending an FCA Camp.

No matter what you choose to do, those kinds of group-relational activities will:

- Allow players to see the coaches away from the sport and personalize that relationship
- Show players that all of them have a place on the team
- Help players see what they can accomplish in life when they work together
- Create a bond among the players that will produce loyalty on the field of competition and friendships that will last beyond their playing days

Another powerful time when team cohesion takes place is when someone on the team or someone close to the team dies. When young people are faced with this kind of tragic reality, they start to talk to each other. They start to lean on each other like never before. The team goes on a group outing to the funeral. And then the rest of the season is usually dedicated to that individual's memory. A team that experiences tragedy will logically have a heightened sense of unity and loyalty. It will always play at a higher level.

But it shouldn't take death to bring a team together. As coaches, let's take intentional steps that will allow for team cohesion to develop organically and positively. Let's do our best to coach these principles into our team instead.

Getting It Together

There are many ways a team can come together and strengthen its foundation. But it's up to you, the coach, to make it happen. Here are some examples of what other coaches just like you have done to promote team cohesion through group-relational activities.

Stirring the Pot

One high school basketball coach told us about an annual canoeing trip that always brings his players closer together. Before they leave, each player is asked to bring some canned vegetables from home. The coach brings a big pot from the school along with some beef stock.

The team usually leaves on a Friday afternoon and then enjoys the rest of whatever daylight is available to ride down the river. That first night, they warm up the stew while setting up their tents. The weather is usually hot and humid. Sometimes it even rains. As the kids fill up their bowls, they tend to complain about the poor conditions and the stew, which is barely touched.

At the end of the second day, the team eats a little more than the previous meal. The conversation picks up and the kids no longer seem to mind their less-than-desirable living quarters. The next morning, the players finish off the rest of the stew for breakfast and enthusiastically talk about how good it tastes. The coach never ceases to be amazed at the drastic change in attitude between the first day and the third day.

Over a short period of time, camaraderie is forged as these teammates stick it out together. They have learned to deal with their circumstances. This single group-relational activity sets the tone for team cohesion throughout the upcoming season.

Mentoring in the Middle

At Wheaton College, head women's basketball coach Melissa Hodgdon annually encourages her players to serve the community through various efforts that include food drives and youth coaching. During the 2012-2013 season, the team initiated a mentoring program with the Norton Middle School eighth-grade girls' basketball team.

In the month of September, team members hosted weekly sessions that sharpened the youngsters' skills. But away from the court, each player was assigned a buddy with whom they set athletic, academic and lifestyle goals. It was common to see Wheaton players attending Norton games and vice versa.

And that's not all the Wheaton athletes did. They also worked with the Heller's Angels Special Olympics basketball team; they partnered with the DJ Dream Fund, a non-profit organization designed to help young people through athletics and wellness programs; and sent letters to wounded soldiers at Walter Reed Hospital.

> "[Community service] has always been an integral part of our program," Hodgdon said. "I just feel that character is a big part of your growth as a student and as a student-athlete. Giving back to the community is a big piece of that."[3]

Picking Up the Pieces

In March 2012, four tornadoes blew through southeastern Kentucky. Dozens of homes were destroyed and 20 people were killed. In the aftermath, a group of 30 football players and four coaches from Madison Southern High School traveled to Laurel County to help with the cleanup.

The team spent the day in a town called East Bernstadt where a mobile home had been thrown "across the road, through the trees, and down a large wooded hill." Head Coach Jon Clark recalls feeling that the task seemed impossible. But the young men worked tirelessly for eight hours and left the area completely clean. They also managed to "pull the entire frame of the house back up the hill." The team finished off its day of service by running a barbed wire fence line to keep the horses safely away from dangerous materials that had been left in a nearby field.[4]

Going to Church

Coach Bobby Bowden used to do something unusual with all of his teams. He took them to church. Before he signed an athlete to play for the Seminoles, he would write a letter to the parents and let them know that they were going to attend church together as a team two times during each academic year. One of the churches would be a predominantly white church and the other would be a predominantly black church.

"I wanted them to see they were welcome no matter what the color of their skin," Coach Bowden once explained.

In his 34 years at Florida, he only had two parents ask him not to include their son, and he didn't. Ironically, those requests came from Christian families. Even though Coach Bowden never took the team to his home church, he assumed those dissenting parents were concerned he was proselytizing them. That was never the case. In addition to creating the foundation for racial unity, he found it equally important to demonstrate the spiritual benefits of church attendance.

Going to Camp

For those working in the public high school system, attending church together as a team is not likely an option. However, another way to enhance your team's spiritual unity is through FCA Camp. A few years into my tenure at East Ridge High School, Coach Bud O'Hara and I decided to start our own FCA Team Camp. Bud called three of his friends to help and together we put together an event that lasted three days and two nights.

That first year, there was just a small collection of teams. Seven years into it, it had increased to over 3,000 football players from all over central Florida. In fact, as it began to grow, we passed it off to the local FCA staff so that they could better handle the administrative duties that had far surpassed anything we could have ever imagined.

There are some coaches in the area who set their calendars around that FCA Camp. They would cancel every other event in the season rather than miss out on this vital piece of their team-building plans. The camp brings a team together in a way that nothing else can and creates a bond that will last beyond the field of play.

These are just a few examples of how some coaches created group-relational opportunities that bonded their athletes together. Do you have a strategy for team cohesion? If you don't, take these stories as the inspiration to set out on a team-bonding journey of your own.

From Last Place to First Place

When Jesus traveled with His team, it was commonplace for them to walk long distances and then settle in for the evening around a campfire or in someone's home. He would fellowship with them after a day of fishing or talk with them over a meal. During these times, He taught them principles that would impact them at both the individual- and group-relational levels.

After one particular day of travel, they arrived in a town called Capernaum, where they found a place to stay for the night. Along the way, Jesus had quietly observed some conversation between the disciples. He questioned them about it as they settled in to their new surroundings:

> "What were you arguing about on the way?" But they were silent, because on the way they had been arguing with one another about who was the greatest. Sitting down, He called the Twelve and said to them, "If anyone wants to be first, he must be last of all and servant of all" (Mark 9:33-35, *HCSB*).

Even in that day, the idea of achieving greatness by becoming someone's servant was *not* a popular concept. This has become even truer in the modern sports culture where winning is the predominant goal of most athletes and teams. But that is exactly what Jesus was suggesting.

||||||||||||||||||||||||||||||||||||||||||||||||||||||||||||||||||||||||||||||||||||||||||||||||||||||

If you want to be in first place, you must first
submit yourself to last place.

||||||||||||||||||||||||||||||||||||||||||||||||||||||||||||||||||||||||||||||||||||||||||||||||||||||

What does becoming a servant mean for your team? Does this mean you shouldn't strive to win a conference championship? Does this mean you shouldn't push your athletes to perform at a high level? Does this mean you should prefer to finish in last place rather than in first place?

No. As we discussed in the first chapter, God wants our best. He desires us to be excellent in everything we do (see Col. 3:23).

What Jesus was telling the disciples (and us) is that true greatness in God's eyes is only achieved when we serve others and do so with a spirit of humility.

And when your athletes truly embrace the concept of serving others, it will have a profound effect on team cohesion. Players will bring that attitude of service into the locker room. They will take it with them onto the practice field and the field of competition. They will have each other's backs. They will give a better effort and that effort will be the result of their desire to serve their teammates. It will produce a sense of loyalty that, as Coach Wooden said, "forges individuals into a team" and "moves teams toward great achievements."

So what is your strategy? It's never too late to put together a group-relational plan that will drastically improve your team cohesion, and, more important, give your athletes an experience that will forever change their worldview.

TRAINING TIME

1. How would you describe the general quality of the relationships within your current team?
2. Can you describe a time when your team's desire to win created an unhealthy atmosphere? If so, what were some of the individual and group characteristics that manifested themselves and how did they threaten team cohesion? How did you respond?

3. What are some things you have done in the community to promote the group-relational aspect within your team?

4. What is your game plan to get your athletes together away from the sports environment so that they can enjoy time together while serving others for a good cause? How would you rate the results of those efforts?

5. How did Jesus redefine "greatness"? Why do you think His definition is so difficult for today's sports culture to embrace? In what ways do you think promoting and cultivating an atmosphere of humility would contribute to greater team cohesion among your players?

PRAYER

Lord, help me to coach in such a way that my players will be inspired to serve others on the team and others outside of the team. Give me creative ideas that will allow them to develop into the servant leaders that You have called them to be. Bond us together with Your love during those times of service and during our times of fellowship together. Help us all to better understand what it means to truly be great in Your eyes, and to strive for that greatness with a spirit of meekness and humility.

Notes

1. John Wooden and Jay Carty, *The Pyramid of Success* (Ventura, CA: Regal Books, 2009), p. 51.
2. John Wooden and Jay Carty, *Coach Wooden One-on-One* (Ventura, CA: Regal Books, 2003), p. 66.
3. "Basketball Team's Goal Is Helping Others," *Wheaton Quarterly*, Spring 2013. http://wheatoncollege.edu/quarterly/2013/03/26/basketball-teams-goal-helping (accessed March 2014).
4. "Football Teams Serving Others in Need," *Sports Leader*, March 21, 2012. http://www.sportsleader.org/2012/03/football-teams-serving-others-in-need (accessed March 2014).

15

LEGACY OF LOVE

In so many aspects of the athletic experience, confidence truly is the key to success. But what happens next has even longer-term implications. Confidence eventually turns into something we will identify as attribution. This allows for athletes to first develop the "confident mindset" and ultimately graduate into a deeper level of confidence called the "optimistic mindset."

Let's dive a little deeper into the second dimension and discover some ways that we can leave a life-changing mark on the young people within our circle of influence.

The Confident Mindset

In chapter 10, we talked about three keys to building confidence in your athletes:

- Performance accomplishments (reminding them of past successes)
- Vicarious experiences (showing them the successes of others)
- Verbal persuasion (encouraging them with positive reinforcement and affirmation)

As you continue to utilize these powerful tools, you will begin to see a change take place throughout your team. Athletes will begin to adopt what we call the confident mindset. There are three distinct components related to what is also referred to as the "Attribution Theory."

1. *Internal attribution*: This is when the athlete takes responsibility for factors under their control. It is the first step towards the confident mindset. They want to do things well. They want to care about others. They want to hustle and give their best because they want to serve their teammates.

2. *External attribution*: This is when the athlete no longer blames himself or herself for aspects of their performance that are beyond their control. It becomes evident when an athlete is no longer shaken by his own failure or the failures of others around him. They are no longer negatively impacted by less than optimal circumstances, such as bad weather, poor field conditions or a hostile playing environment. An athlete who exercises external attribution will believe he or she can perform a task even when others don't think they can.

   According to Shawn Byler, Ph.D., of Momentum Performance Development, performance is "directly related to how an athlete feels about himself/herself. Your athletes will learn faster, perform better, and have fewer practice problems when you, the coach, use techniques to catapult the athlete toward confidence and high self-esteem."

3. *Global attribution*: This is when an athlete believes that his or her successes will generalize to all areas of their lives. For instance, the kid who struggles with academics will begin to believe that he can pass math class or be able to qualify for college or be able to have a successful life as a businessperson or whatever profession he might choose.

For the longest time, I failed to realize how deeply I was mired in the first dimension. Like so many first-dimension coaches, I only cared about eligibility. But second-dimension coaches care about academics and college admissions. If a 3.5 student drops to 3.0 or 2.8, a first-dimension coach won't take the time to deal with him or her, because they're still eligible. On the other hand, a second-dimension coach will contribute to that athlete's global attribution by stepping in and helping them do better.

For an athlete with a confident mindset, the world is suddenly much bigger than just sports. It's interesting to note that many of our modern U.S. Presidents had strong ties to athletics. Through sports, men like Gerald Ford, Ronald Reagan, George W. Bush, George H.W. Bush, John F. Kennedy and Barack Obama achieved internal, external and global attribution to the point of believing that they could become the leader of the free world.

The Optimistic Mindset

If we are only concerned about how an athlete's confidence will help our team perform better, then we are still stuck in the first dimension. But a second-dimension coach can see the big picture. A second-dimension coach understands the concept of legacy and how his influence over an athlete can change individual lives and entire communities. Therefore, the ultimate goal should be to help athletes achieve what we call the optimistic mindset.

Whereas the confident mindset is indentified by global attribution (the belief that success in athletics will transfer to other areas of life), the optimistic mindset takes one giant leap further to the most powerful kind of confidence.

It's called *stable attribution* and it fosters certainty in one's ability and efforts by helping that person believe that his or her success in the present will continue to ensure success in the future. In other words, athletes who achieve stable attribution will become stable human beings and positive contributors to society well beyond their sports careers.

This is the power you have as a coach. Because of your words, you can help an athlete believe that, not only can they do other things in their life well (global attribution), but that they also can enjoy sustained success as they move into married life, family life, professional life and community life (stable attribution).

Every training and competitive experience offers information that can either build up or harm an athlete's confidence. Everything out of our mouth and all of our actions *will* make an impact. We can lead our athletes to that optimistic mindset where they can then become skilled at recognizing positive feedback and distancing themselves from negative feedback. This is something that you as the coach can teach and model for your athletes.

Take it from someone who has gone through the process: Both you *and* your athletes will be changed. But it requires building your program on a foundation that utilizes second-dimension principles. Jesus talked about the importance of a solid foundation in one of His parables:

> Therefore everyone who hears these words of mine and puts them into practice is like a wise man who built his house on the rock. The rain came down, the streams rose, and the winds blew and beat against that house; yet it did not fall, because it

had its foundation on the rock. But everyone who hears these words of mine and does not put them into practice is like a foolish man who built his house on sand. The rain came down, the streams rose, and the winds blew and beat against that house, and it fell with a great crash (Matt. 17:24-27).

Jesus was talking here about two lifestyle choices. The first man built his house (or life) on a solid foundation. That house was able to withstand the storm (or troubles). The second man built his house (or life) on a shaky foundation. His house was destroyed when the storm (or troubles) violently came through.

Think about your team in terms of these two men. Is your team built on a solid rock of confidence that is progressing through the various levels of attribution (internal, external, global and stable)? Or is your team built on a sandy foundation full of athletes whose confidence is easily shaken?

||||||||||||||||||||||||||||||||||||||||||||||||||||||||||||||||||||||||||||||||||||||||||||||||||||

Confidence is an issue that often requires us to
pay attention to the athlete's heart. And that means
reinforcing what is good and right.

||||||||||||||||||||||||||||||||||||||||||||||||||||||||||||||||||||||||||||||||||||||||||||||||||||

Yes, we as coaches need to fix what is wrong with our athletes. Some of those things are done in the first dimension, but other things need to be addressed in the second dimension.

Confidence vs. Arrogance

You've heard it said before, and it's really true: There's a very thin line between confidence and arrogance. As you work on strategies to build up your team's confidence, it's important, especially as a Christian coach, not to allow confidence and optimism to subtly morph into arrogance and cockiness.

That's why you should, while building up confidence, simultaneously teach and model humility to your coaching staff and to your team. This can be exhibited through other character traits, such as graciousness (in victory *and* in defeat), patience, kindness and gentleness, and through acts of service.

Scripture reiterates the value of humility time and again, including these words from the apostle Peter:

> Clothe yourselves, all of you, with humility toward one another, for "God opposes the proud but gives grace to the humble." Humble yourselves, therefore, under the mighty hand of God so that at the proper time he may exalt you, casting all your anxieties on him, because he cares for you (1 Pet. 5:5-7).

Former NFL head coach Tony Dungy is a modern day example of what it looks like to have unwavering confidence while maintaining a genuine heart of humility. Even when he was hoisting the Super Bowl trophy amid the hoopla of an international spotlight, Coach Dungy still made sure to give credit to others and pass the glory along to his Creator. And he always seemed to understand the big picture: that it wasn't about what *he* could get out of the sport, but what others could learn in the present and how they could take that with them into the future.

Our job as coaches is to show players that we're here to make them better players. Yes, there are some personal benefits we're going to get out of it, but if we're in it for personal benefit, we're in it for the wrong reasons. You're a coach to help your team and your players grow. When you see guys grow and you see players get better on the field and you see them mature and gain confidence, that's where you get all of your satisfaction. It's from knowing that you have helped someone.

Legacy of Love

What Coach Dungy is really talking about here is legacy. He's talking about truly caring about players enough to want to guide them to those life-changing revelations that bring about global and stable attribution—the belief that an athlete can do something well in other areas of his or her life and the belief that he or she can sustain that success over long periods of time.

In his book *InSideOut Coaching*, Joe Erhmann defines legacy this way: "How do I know if I've coached well? Ask me in 20 years."[1]

In other words, once I see what kind of parent, spouse or citizen an athlete becomes, that's when I'll know whether or not I was successful as a coach. When you see sustained successes take place in your athletes' lives, you'll know you are doing something that will last infinitely longer than the euphoric feeling that follows a state championship. Those long-term successes will produce trophies that will never lose their shine. That kind of legacy will stand the test of time and continue even beyond your temporal life here on Earth.

In one of the Bible's most famous passages, Jesus talked to the disciples about the kind of legacy He was going to leave:

> For God so loved the world that he gave his one and only Son, that whoever believes in him shall not perish but have eternal life (John 3:16).

We are not being asked to literally give up our lives for our athletes, but we, in essence, are sacrificially giving of ourselves in an effort to build up their confidence both for short-term athletic success and, more important, for long-term success in life. Coaches are remembered for what they do and say (both the good and the bad).

Earlier in this book, I mentioned a couple of backup receivers who never played much but took very positive experiences from their time with the East Ridge program. One of those young men is Brad Cox. I coached him for three years. At one point, he became frustrated over the lack of playing time and was about to quit the team. But at an FCA Camp, I sat down with him to talk about life and football and whatever topics came to mind. Brad left that camp affirmed both as an athlete and as a person. He stuck it out and is glad that he did.

Brad is now married with two daughters. He sends me a text message about once a week to share something good that's happened in his life. "Coach! I just want to tell you that what I learned from playing football was so awesome!" he once told me.

I don't remember talking to Brad about raising children. Our coaching staff didn't break down film on the finer points of being a husband. But somehow he took away invaluable lessons that have helped him have a productive, fulfilling life.

Another example of attribution can be found in a young man named Edwin Bonilla. I didn't coach Edwin but he was one of my students at UCF. His father was from Cuba and his mother was from Nicaragua. Edwin wanted to be a baseball coach but English was his second language. It was a constant struggle for him to get through his classes. I did my best to motivate him and keep his confidence up.

We placed Edwin with a 3D Coach for his practicum experience so that he could see firsthand these principles in action. He became the first member of his family to graduate from college and later earned his teaching certificate. Edwin moved to Miami where he was hired as the head baseball coach at a predominantly Hispanic high school. He is now married and has a son.

"I am so thankful for what I learned in the 3Dimensional Coaching classes," Edwin recently wrote to me. "It has made all the difference in my life."

You get it all when you lead using these second-dimension principles. Your athletes will get it on the field. But more important, you will create attribution that will have a long-term positive impact on the rest of their lives.

||||||||||||||||||||||||||||||||||||||||||||||||||||||||||||||||||||||||||||||||||||||||||||||||

Your athletes will remember you as someone
who loved them, gave yourself up for them and
allowed them to do life better because of the
biblical concepts you taught them.

||||||||||||||||||||||||||||||||||||||||||||||||||||||||||||||||||||||||||||||||||||||||||||||||

TRAINING TIME

1. Review the attributes of the confident mindset. What is your strategy for taking your athletes from internal attribution all the way to global attribution?

2. Can you share an example when you saw an athlete reach global attribution and begin to believe they could have success beyond sports? What do you think helped him or her achieve this?

3. What are some things that might hinder an athlete from adopting an optimistic mindset? What are some ways that you might be able to help them believe that they can achieve long-term success in life and maintain stable attribution?

4. Read 1 Peter 5:5-7. What do you believe is the connection between humility and confidence? Why is it important to model and teach humility to your athletes?

5. How important is legacy to you? What might fruit from a "legacy of love" look like in relation to your coaching career?

PRAYER

Lord, give me a strategy to help my athletes adopt both the confident mindset and the optimistic mindset. Help me instill in them a godly confidence that promotes humility and rejects arrogance. My desire is to leave a legacy of love that will outlast my time on this Earth and produce eternal fruit that always seeks to glorify Your name.

Note

1. Joe Ehrmann and Gregory Jordan, *InSide Out Coaching* (New York: Simon & Schuster, 2011).

16

THE JOURNEY

So much of what I've learned about 3Dimensional Coaching has forced me to buck against human nature and the broken sports culture. It's been a long, hard journey of discovery that has led me to this realization.

Strangely, as a long-time Christian, I've had the answer right in front of me every step of the way. It just took me 30 years to see the connection between one of the apostle Paul's most famous teachings and my tumultuous adventure as a coach.

> Do not conform to the pattern of this world, but be transformed by the renewing of your mind. Then you will be able to test and approve what God's will is—His good, pleasing and perfect will (Rom. 12:2).

When God placed a desire in my heart to coach, it was "His good, pleasing and perfect will" for my life. But I made the mistake of conforming to the world's view of what coaching was supposed to look like and became confused in the process. Instead, I should have allowed the Holy Spirit to transform me and renew my mind. Thankfully, I eventually got to that place and it completely transformed me as a coach, as a husband, as a parent, and as a follower of Christ.

Good Decisions

One of my closest friends went through that same transformation process late in his coaching career. It was incredible to see how he was able to use his past struggles to help his players embark on a spiritual journey of their own.

After the first game of the season, he gathered his team in the locker room. It was no different than what most coaches do. He gave the team a little pep talk, discussed some general points about the game, and then went through a few administrative items.

Most of you can relate to that scenario. In some cases, it might include a parting phrase that coaches often use before dismissing the team: "Make good decisions this weekend!"

Make good decisions.

What does that mean to a kid? Maybe they don't know what it means to make a good decision.

Here's what my friend told his team about making good decisions: "Let me just tell you about myself," he opened. "Believe it or not, I was your age at one time."

The kids laughed at the thought of their coach as a teenager.

"I made the varsity football team when I was in tenth grade," he said. "I badly wanted to be liked and to be a part of the team. So I started drinking on the weekends because that's what some of the varsity kids did. When I went to college, I played ball, I partied and I drank a lot. The alcohol started to consume me."

By now, the room was completely silent. No one was moving around. After a brief pause, the coach continued.

"When I got out of college, I got married and became a pretty successful coach, but the alcohol began to control me. After many years of marriage, my wife couldn't take it anymore. She left me. A lot of you know that I'm divorced, but I also have sons. I lost my marriage and I nearly lost my kids. And that's why I just want you to know that your coach is an alcoholic."

All eyes were fixated on the coach. He had more to say. "When my wife walked out on me six years ago, I had to do something. So I went and got help. I want you to know that I've been sober for six years. It's been a difficult journey. I really understand who I am and the importance of what God has done for me. But it's lonely over the weekends. I really get tempted when I go home and I don't have anyone with me. So I'm going to change it up this year. Instead of me telling you to make good decisions, I'm going to ask you guys to not drink this weekend. I'm asking that you say no to alcohol. And then I'm going to ask you how you did on Monday. But I also want *you* to ask *me* how I did on Monday."

After the coach gave his talk, an amazing thing happened. Every Monday morning, his players would periodically stop by before first period. They would knock and peek into his office.

"Hey, Coach," they'd say. "How'd you do?"

For the next few years, that coach had to answer to 60 varsity kids every Monday morning. He created accountability for himself and his players. Prior to that speech, his program had dealt with major alcohol problems. But after he opened up to his team, there are no longer any consistent alcohol problems.

The Role of a Coach

For many years, that coach—like myself and countless others—was trapped in the first dimension. He didn't understand what it meant to capture the heart of the athlete in the second dimension. And he certainly didn't understand that there was a greater purpose to coaching than winning games and stockpiling trophies.

But on that day in the locker room, he was able to speak courageously and transparently before those young men. His journey, like mine, was much more difficult than it needed to be, but thankfully, he had finally begun to understand his influence as a coach. He now knew that his purpose in life was to reach those young people in a meaningful way and impact them at a much deeper and more spiritual level.

That is the true role of a coach—to take athletes somewhere they can't go on their own. In the first dimension, this means teaching them physical skills and training principles that help them achieve their potential on the field of play. In the second dimension, this means dealing with issues of the heart, such as emotions, confidence, motivation and team cohesion.

The third dimension is different. This is where the highest level of coaching takes place. It is defined by the connection between body, mind and spirit—or *holism*. This dimension encompasses spiritual issues such as character, identity, purpose and significance.

If you want to be effective at coaching in the third dimension, you must first deal with those deeper issues within your own heart. As I said earlier in this book, you can't be a tour guide to a land where you've never been. You must first go on a spiritual journey and discover that your purpose is much bigger than what today's sports culture portrays.

Discovering Truth

After I finished my doctoral degree, the University of Central Florida approached me about the work I had done. They were struggling to place a large group of young adults who were interested in pursuing coaching as a career. The administration had no idea where to go with the concept. How do you educate coaches?

I received a grant from the state of Florida and wrote a degree program for UCF. It has since become a very large program with over 1,000 students. It was humbling to be a small part of what it has now become. Ironically, this is actually what I do for a living. I teach undergraduates and graduate students who are interested in the coaching profession. I can't help but think back to my junior year in college when the academic advisor infamously asked me, "What do you *really* want to do?"

Because UCF is a public university, I only share the research and not the biblical components of the 3Dimensional concept. I am able to talk about the greater purpose of coaching in a general context, but I have my limitations. That's why it is so important for me to share what God's Word has to say in other forums, such as this book and through my work with FCA Coaches Academy.

So what is the Bible saying to those of us who at some level have the title "Coach"?

First of all, you have to make a decision. Either the Bible is true and applies to you as a coach, or it doesn't apply to you at all. You have to either take a look at what Jesus had to say, or get on with your career. You have to be willing to embrace Jesus' radical claim, or keep doing things the way you've always done them.

I am the way and the truth and the life. No one comes to the Father except through me (John 14:6).

If you're not quite ready to jump on board with that Scripture, then there is still some solid research that can help make coaching a more enjoyable experience. But the funny thing about research is that it always reveals truth, and as I went through the 3Dimensional Coaching research, it became increasingly clear and conclusive that

Jesus had coached His team in a special way. Maybe that's why He had 12 guys. Maybe He wanted to give us a living example of what it means to take a group of individuals and coach them really well.

Not long ago, I conducted a survey of coaches across the nation. While it was not an empirical study, it did yield some interesting results. We asked this question:

Does the Bible affect how you coach?

Less than 5 percent of the coaches answered yes. Yet much more than 5 percent of the nation's coaches claim Christianity as their faith. So either the Bible is not true and has zero relevance, or the vast majority of coaches are ignorant about what it says. For many years, I fell into that latter category. It took me awhile to figure this out, but every time I read a journal article about the best way to coach today's young people, it can be linked directly back to how Jesus coached *His* team!

Going on a Journey

The third dimension is about your journey. I don't know where you are in this journey. You might be far away from Christ. You might think, *I'd like to find out about this Jesus*. Some of you, like myself, are believers, but you don't realize the power and presence of what He wants to do in your everyday life and the empowerment He can give. All I needed was a partner—a coach in my own life. Some of you understand this and what you're reading simply affirms who you are. I praise God for you. Keep going! Keep making a difference!

Wherever you might be in the journey, consider this: If you want the best for your athletes, you must first want the best for yourself.

You must become whole if you want to truly affect your athletes and honor their spirit and purpose.

To do that, you have to get past the conforming pressures that come from within the broken sports culture. Sports are great if you're just trying to measure yourself or your kids or your athletes against others. Winning is the ultimate measure within that context. But winning is never enough. It is temporary at best; it never satisfies long term.

I can't imagine what it would be like if every coach who professes Christ as their Savior actually made Him the Lord of their coaching. From youth sports all the way to the professional ranks, we would collectively experience a transformation of the culture!

Whether you're just starting the journey or you're several years into it, the key is once again found in the teachings of Jesus, the Master Coach: One day, Jesus was with His team when some religious leaders of the day tried to take Him off His game with some tricky questions. These men were well versed in the Ten Commandments and the 400 or so Pharisaic laws.

"Which of these commandments is the greatest?" one philosopher asked.

With the proverbial 25-second play clock running, Jesus deftly summarized all of those teachings into the two most important:

"Love the Lord your God with all your heart and with all your soul and with all your mind and with all your strength." The second is this: "Love your neighbor as yourself" (Mark 12:29-30).

Does that sound familiar? It should. Jesus tells the people that the most important thing they need to do in order to please God is to *love* Him with all of their heart, soul, mind and strength. Those are the three dimensions: strength (first dimension), mind (second dimension), and soul and heart (third dimension).

Jesus taught in the three dimensions. Nothing has changed. We say it's a new theory, but the research is only unveiling the oldest teachings known to man. And they are available to all coaches as we go on this spiritual journey of discovery—a journey that will transform us from the inside out and allow us to have an eternal impact on our athletes.

TRAINING TIME

1. Read Romans 12:2. In light of what we've discussed in this book, describe what it might look like to "conform to the pattern of this world" as a coach. On the other hand, how might it look to be "transformed by the renewing of your mind"?
2. Has your definition of the role of a coach changed as you've read this book? Explain.
3. What do you think it means to be on a spiritual journey as a coach?
4. Which spiritual issues discussed (character, identity, purpose and significance) do you struggle with the most in your heart?
5. How do you think addressing those issues will help you better serve the emotional and spiritual needs of your athletes?

PRAYER

Lord, reveal to me the spiritual issues that are holding me back in my relationship with You and keeping me from leading my athletes to an understanding of true significance and purpose. Make me whole so that I can be wholly used as a vessel for Your glory.

17

BREAKFAST WITH CHAMPIONS

At six o'clock on any given Tuesday morning in the Clermont, Florida, area, about a dozen high school coaches can be seen occupying two or three tables in the back of the local IHOP. But there's something a little bit different about this meeting. You won't hear any discussion of the previous week's big game. You won't see anyone poring over a two-inch thick playbook. And most important, you won't feel the stress that often accompanies a stereotypical gathering of athletic tacticians.

What you might find instead is a group of guys celebrating each other's personal successes, consoling each other's disappointments, reading the Bible or a devotional book, praying for each other, and sharing stories about their shared journey as coaches. You'll almost always find me sitting right in the middle of it all.

It all started back in 2001 when I embarked on this journey with Coach Bud O'Hara. I had just joined his coaching staff at East Ridge High School and we wanted to meet once a week to discuss what biblical coaching might look like. Eventually the group doubled in size and eventually grew to the point where between 8 and 12 coaches were meeting on a regular basis. It's the most powerful thing I've ever done in all my years as a coach.

Our weekly breakfast meeting has become a safe haven. Our only rule is that we can't talk about football. No *X*s and *O*s. Instead, we talk about God's Word. We use devotional materials like Chip Ingram's

R12 Coach series or *Legacy Builders* by Rod Olson. The FCA Coach's Bible has been our most consistent resource. Sometimes we talk about second-dimension issues and sometimes we talk about our own personal struggles with things like marriage, parenting and personal finances.

We have celebrated births, marriages and promotions. We have suffered through sickness, injuries and even the death of family members. We have prayed for athletes and put into action outreach efforts for hurting kids on our teams. We have collected money among ourselves to help players' family members who might be struggling financially because of divorce or an economic downturn. We have seen real miracles take place in all areas of life. It has created wholeness and oneness within the group.

But the only reason we even knew about these issues is because we took the time to meet and discuss second- and third-dimension issues and strategies. For the first several years, we didn't even use those terms, but that's what we were doing. We were talking about our relationships and opening up about our spiritual journeys.

And all of this happened because two broken coaches who loved sports and loved God just wanted to seek a better way.

The 3D Coaching Revolution

Mark Woolum is the head football coach at South Lake High School. Bud O'Hara mentored him at East Ridge before he took that position. I was there during that time and saw Mark change under Bud's 3Dimensional Coaching style. It was unlike anything he had ever experienced before.

"I just can't believe how it changed my way of thinking," Mark told me during one of our breakfast meetings. "Under the old system, we'd have a high school game on Friday night and then our staff would go to Denny's and we'd watch the sun come up—still talking about what to do to get better. It was always about outworking your opponent. What did we do from 10 at night to 6 A.M. at Denny's? We were so infatuated with trying to get good in the first dimension, and if we lost, we were killing ourselves trying to figure out why."

How did that affect his family?

"Jeff," he said, "we all about lost our families. All of us."

Mark's story is typical of so many young coaches today. Coaching in the first dimension almost always means putting in 16 hours a day under the banner of this noble thing we call *work ethic*—all for the sake of building a winning program. Ironically, the word "ethic" is too often a disposable part of the equation.

"We would do whatever it took," Mark added. "Sometimes that meant covering up a kid's behavior. They would get in trouble in class and we were there to enable them and bail them out so they could line up on Friday night and play. The more we worked, the worse the attitude of the kids and coaches would become. When we started losing a few games, we had to spend more hours coming up with game plans and schemes. It wore us out. It took the fun out of the game."

When Mark started attending a breakfast meeting that Bud and I were leading, he saw something different. He didn't fully understand it at first, but eventually he started to see the big picture. It was in an environment of transparency that Mark experienced significant personal and spiritual growth.

We've seen that same thing happen in both Christian and non-Christian coaches. We've seen Christians grow closer in their relationship with the Lord and we've seen non-Christians take that first step of their faith journey. It amazes me when I think of the hundreds of young people, parents and school administrators who have witnessed this better way of coaching. And we've only just begun to see the 3D Coaching revolution start to slowly spread across the nation.

As more 3D Coaches begin to emerge, I believe there will be a noticeable change on campuses and in ballparks, arenas and stadiums everywhere. That's because when you walk into a 3D Coach's office, you can sense the joy and excitement. When you step onto those football fields, baseball diamonds, tennis courts, basketball floors or whatever sports facility it might be, there will be a palpable difference in those places. There will be peace and contentment.

That's where I am today. My journey hasn't always been pretty. I was born to coach. That was my calling. But I allowed the pull of this world to take me away from the thing I so dearly love. God's grace is unbelievable. Not only did He provide a way to spend eternity with Him someday in heaven, but he also brought me back home to the place I was supposed to be in the first place.

Now I get to teach young people who want to coach. I get to travel with FCA, one of the best organizations in the world. And finally, I *still* get to coach high school kids. In fact, in late 2013, my son Cameron was hired to be the head football coach at Lake Highland Prep School in Orlando. That previous summer, I had spent two days with that school's coaches talking about 3D Coaching. The clinic was so impactful that the school administrators later expressed to me their desire to hire 3D Coaches.

And guess who gets to be Cameron's offensive coordinator?

I'm excited about the next phase of my journey. I'm even more excited to see how many others out there—including you reading this book—will be willing to join me. Today's athletes are looking for someone to enter into their lives. The broken sports culture can be transformed. And *you* are the key!

TRAINING TIME

1. Do you have a group of peers who you meet with or talk to on a regular basis and with whom you share similar biblical values? If so, how has that benefited you and the group?
2. If more coaches embraced these 3Dimensional principles, how do you think the complexion of your team might change? Your school? Your community?
3. What are some things that you can start to do that might help action plan and take the first step today.

PRAYER

Lord, place other 3D Coaches in my life who will encourage me, pray for me and mentor me as I embark on this journey. Give me the boldness to step out in faith and lead a revolution within my team, my school and my community. I want to see You glorified as lives are changed forever.

ACKNOWLEDGMENTS

Why anybody would want to read this book about me is beyond comprehension. My story is so ordinary, but it has become extraordinary only by a humble desire to serve the greatest influencers of the twenty-first century—coaches. My calling is to help them identify their life-giving and eternal purpose. If this book helps but one start this journey, then it was worth all the time and effort. So with this, thanks to those at the National Support Center of the Fellowship of Christian Athletes for shepherding this project: Dan Britton, Shea Vailes and Jeff Martin.

To my colleagues at Florida State University and University of Central Florida: Dr. Beverly Yerg, Dr. Mike Kehoe, Jeff Biddle, and Bill Kuminka. Thank you for helping me put order and depth to the transformational teaching of 3Dimensional Coaching.

As a teacher and a coach, I enjoy the engagement of faces much more than spending time with the written word. Writing a book is a strain for me and could not have come to fruition without Chad Bonham and Lance Griffin putting pen to paper. A special thanks needs to be given to Jeanne Battersby as she has served so faithfully and enthusiastically as our program assistant at the university and special assistant with me as related to my duties with FCA.

Thanks to the real men in my life who have allowed a bond of transparent hearts to be shared with one another. To be real, every coach needs a safe haven. This is where my transformational journey is truly engaged and enhanced. Thanks, guys: John Harmeling, Ken Smith, David Howell, Mark Wilbanks, Tommy Bowden, Bud O'Hara, Tim Hancock, Del Wright, John Brost, Wes Simmons, Mark Hull, Terry McEwen and Scott Armatti.

Finally, a special thanks to all the players, coaches, administrators and academicians I have had the honor of doing life with during the past 30-plus years. Life is a journey. Embrace and engage it *daily* and experience an eternal purpose of joy!

Jeff Duke

IMPACTING THE WORLD FOR CHRIST THROUGH SPORTS

FELLOWSHIP OF CHRISTIAN ATHLETES

Since 1954, the Fellowship of Christian Athletes has challenged athletes and coaches to impact the world for Jesus Christ. FCA is cultivating Christian principles in local communities nationwide by encouraging, equipping, and empowering others to serve as examples and make a difference. FCA reaches more than 2 million people annually on the professional, college, high school, junior high and youth levels. Through FCA's Four Cs of Ministry—coaches, campus, camps, and community—and the shared passion for athletics and faith, lives are changed for current and future generations.

Fellowship of Christian Athletes
8701 Leeds Road • Kansas City, MO 64129
www. fca.org • fca@fca.org • 1-800-289-0909

COMPETITORS FOR CHRIST

Fellowship of Christian Athletes Coach's Mandate

Pray as though nothing of eternal value is going
to happen in my athletes' lives unless God does it.

Prepare each practice and game as giving "my utmost for His highest."

Seek not to be served by my athletes for personal gain, but seek
to serve them as Christ served the church.

Be satisfied not with producing a good record, but with producing good athletes.

Attend carefully to my private and public walk with God, knowing that the
athlete will never rise to a standard higher than that being lived by the coach.

Exalt Christ in my coaching, trusting the Lord will then draw athletes to Himself.

Desire to have a growing hunger for God's Word, for personal
obedience, for fruit of the spirit and for saltiness in competition.

Depend solely upon God for transformation—one athlete at a time.

Preach Christ's word in a Christ-like demeanor, on and off the field of competition.

Recognize that it is impossible to bring glory to both myself
and Christ at the same time.

Allow my coaching to exude the fruit of the Spirit,
thus producing Christ-like athletes.

Trust God to produce in my athletes His chosen purposes,
regardless of whether the wins are readily visible.

Coach with humble gratitude, as one privileged to be God's coach.

Dr. Jeff Duke is the foremost expert regarding the cultural influence on the coaching profession in our society. He has developed and authored the "3Dimensional Pyramid of Coaching Success" concept that has revolutionized the sport coaching landscape. Dr. Duke has coached five sports including football, basketball, track and field, cross-country and tennis; and has directly suppervised over 200 coaches in 17 different sports. His coaching experience encompasses youth level through the professional ranks, coupled with a multi-year stint as an assistant football coach at Florida State University under legendary coach, Bobby Bowden.

Dr. Duke is highly sought after to lead workshops, seminars, and training on the "cultural influence of the sport coach" throughout Europe and the Americas. He spent eight years as an international expert on coaching education development pre/post the Atlanta Olympic Games. His doctoral research (Florida State University) created baseline data on how to analyze proficient elite level coaching methods. Today, you will find Dr. Duke traveling weekly across the United States, leading and facilitating workshops with the adolescent sport coaching culture on becoming "3Dimensional Coaches."

Dr. Duke is available to conduct professional service trainings on the following topics:

- **Motivation**
- **Mental Imagery**
- **Focus**
- **Emotions**
- **Intensity**
- **Team Cohesion**
- **Confidence**
- **Goal Setting**

For more information, log onto www.3dimensionalcoaching.com

**Scan to "like"
3Dimensional Coaching**

**Scan to "follow"
@3DCoaches**

3Dimensional Coaching

Research shows that coaches who coach in all 3Dimensions are more likely to produce athletes who:

- learn skills quicker (*more attentive*)

- achieve higher fitness compliance (*work harder*)

- experience shorter rehabilitation (*recover from injury*)

- are more adaptable to new conditions (*"on the road"*)

- possess the freedom to be creative (*"are gamers"*)

- develop deeper relationships with other players and with coaches (*learn life's lessons*)

HEART

PSYCHOLOGY

FUNDAMENTALS

Dr. Jeff Duke, Ed.D.
University of Central Florida

"Coaching the Heart Behind the Jersey"

What is 3Dimensional Coaching™?

The 3Dimensional Coaching™ curriculum is based on extensive research regarding different coaching philosophies and the cultural influence of coaches in the lives of the people they impact.

1st Dimension = Fundamentals (Physical)*
2nd Dimension = Psychology (Mind)
3rd Dimension = Heart (Holism)

Research shows only about 15% of coaches intentionally coach beyond the 1st Dimension.

Why does it matter?

- The social structure of our culture has drastically changed over the past 20 years.

- Research validates the "coach" as the single-most influential authoritative figure in life of today's adolescent.

- 70% of athletes will fail to reach their full potential on and off the field because of 2nd Dimension issues.

What is your 2nd Dimension coaching _strategy_?

▶ Motivation
▶ Confidence
▶ Emotions
▶ Team Cohesion